Thank You!

JIM NEWMAN

That Dog, Don't Hunt

Tales From The
Hunt Camp Porch

A humorous look at the Hunting Culture

A collection of articles published in
The Nipissing Reader from November 2016
to September 2020

◆ FriesenPress

One Printers Way
Altona, MB R0G 0B0
Canada

www.friesenpress.com

Copyright © 2021 by Jim Newman
First Edition — 2021

All rights reserved.

No part of this publication may be reproduced in any form, or by any means, electronic or mechanical, including photocopying, recording, or any information browsing, storage, or retrieval system, without permission in writing from FriesenPress.

ISBN
978-1-5255-9728-2 (Hardcover)
978-1-5255-9727-5 (Paperback)
978-1-5255-9729-9 (eBook)

1. HUMOR, TOPIC, ANIMALS

Distributed to the trade by The Ingram Book Company

ACKNOWLEDGMENTS

I would like to thank Frank and Lizanne Attwood, the publishers of the Nipissing Reader for giving me the opportunity to pen the original articles. And having the patience to endure my constant failure to respect the concept of the term deadline.

To all those individuals that participated in the various focus groups, I want to express my thanks and indebtedness for the giving of your time, reading the rough drafts of the book and offering your suggestions, comments and constructive criticisms.

My wife Judy. I don't know how to thank you. Without your understanding, patience and encouragement of my passion for hunting season there wouldn't be any stories. In keeping with that support Thank you for contributing all the sketches.

GLOSSARY

ATV: All-Terrain Vehicle, also known as a quad, four-track, 4-wheeler—commonly, in our area just called a bike, one of the miracles of technology that extends the ability of aged hunters like me to continue to enjoy the sport.

big red: Honda 200 CC 3-wheel ATV introduced in 1982

bird-shot: A shot gun shell loaded with small lead pellets

Boone & Crocket scale: A method of measuring antlers founded by President Theodore Roosevelt in 1895.

buck shot: A shot gun shell loaded with larger lead balls, usually .333 inches in diameter.

dogger: The hunters trying to drive the game toward the other hunters in the stands or on watches.

game pole: A structure built to hang game on to help preserve and protect it from scavengers.

ground blind: A camouflaged location on the ground concealing the hunter from animals

Hershey Cocaine: Addictive chocolate. Derived from the name of a commercially-produced game attractant, Deer Cocaine.

hunter orange/blaze orange: The hunter orange garment by regulation; it must cover a minimum of 400 square inches (2,580 square centimetres) above the waist and be visible from all sides.

MNRF: Ontario Ministry of Natural Resources and Forestry

Speckle: Small Brook Trout or Speckle Trout found in small streams throughout central Ontario.

run/drive: A method of hunting, simply walking through the bush, with or without dogs, to move deer out of their hiding places and in to the hunters on their watches or stands. Usually into the wind.

side-hill: Along a side of the hill, as apposed to looking up or down.

stalking: A method of hunting, slowly walking stopping and standing, pursuing or approaching stealthily.

Travois: Two joined poles, originally the structure poles from the Teepee, forming a triangle pulled by a horse, dog, or man. formerly used by Plains Indians to carry their lodges and belongings.

tree stands: Elevated, open or enclosed platforms secured to trees to give a better vantage point. Also refers to any structure built to elevate the hunter.

Yogi: Hanna Barbara mischievous bear cartoon character; "Smarter Than The Average Bear." Slang term for a black bear.

Walleye/Pickerel: The same fish, American call it a walleye, Canadians call it a pickerel.

watch / stand: A hunter's best guess location in the bush as to where animals will go.

WMU: Wildlife Management Unit

THE HUNT CAMP PORCH DICTIONARY

Not in alphabetical order, not in my nature to be organized.

Vegetarian: Word used to describe an unsuccessful hunter. Derived from an old Ojibwa word for lousy hunter.

Fisherman/Outright liar: Specific phrase used to describe any fisherman telling tales of his catch. I have been told that fishermen cannot be believed; they are just plain outright liars.

Anti-Hunter: Pronounced sanc·ti·mo·ni·ous – a derogatory adjective meaning, making a show of being morally superior to other people, self-righteous, holier-than-thou, pious, pietistic, moralizing, preachy, smug, superior, and hypocritical.

"That dog don't hunt!": A sarcastic expression used to refer to something that is not likely to happen or to something that is as useless as a hound that won't hunt; for example, my grandfather would tell me to do my chores, and my uncle would chortle, *"That dog don't hunt!"*

lazy wind: According to my Father-in-law this is a wind that is *"so lazy it doesn't go around you but straight through you."*

"It's as true as I'm sitting here" "without a word of a lie": Interchangeable statements; used to clarify that only a slight amount of what I am about to say is true.

"Did I tell you the story" "Do you mind the time" "Well let me tell ya now": Substitute statements for *"I have told this story a thousand times, but I am going to tell it again."*

Swamp Donkey: A scraggly old cow moose

Bullwinkle: Slang term used to describe any bull moose. Derived from the name of a cartoon character.

Swamp buck: A mythical creature seldom seen or harvested. A sly old male deer.

There is a little frost on the pumpkin this morning: Sarcastic statement used in the fall to clarify that it's damned cold.

Meat magnet: Refers to a lucky hunter. Game will come out them no matter what they are doing.

Duck Hunter: The inflicting of punishment on oneself. Wait all year to hunt in the coldest, damp, sleety miserable conditions. Known to look forward to getting up in the middle of the night to go hunting.

Mackinaw coat: An unlined short coat that encourages layering, made of heavy and dense water-repellent woolen cloth, usually a red plaid tartan pattern, double-shouldered with five pockets. Popular with hunters pre-hunter orange. Shrinks if washed or gets wet so you had to wear it till it dried. Origin: the Canadian frontier, logging camps and hunt camps.

"Northern Ontario" (substitute any rural part of Canada) dinner jacket: Reasonably clean Mackinaw jacket. Can be worn, despite your wife's pleas, to all up-scale social events, romantic dinner out with your wife, weddings, or church—any place that calls for formal wear.

Kitchen Bitch: Hunt camp term refers to any hunter at the camp stuck with the cooking, dishes or kitchen duties. *** **HEALTH CANADA WARNING** *** Do not—I repeat: Do NOT—use this term at home when your wife is in the kitchen.

Hot Seat: A toilet seat that is hung up on a nail beside the camp stove or back door to be taken out with you to the outhouse when needed.

Camp Day:
- a. verb: A work day at the camp in the summer or early fall, preparing the camp for the season, doing general repairs, maintaining trails, cutting and splitting firewood etc., where half the gang works, and the other half stands around with a beverage in hand, watching.
- 1. noun: A foul weather day too miserable to go out and hunt. Note, the number of these days increases exponentially as gang members age.
- 2. noun: An in-voluntary quiet day of recovery spent at camp, usually the result of the celebration of harvesting, or even almost harvesting, an animal.

Designated Cook: Refers to hunter that can't shoot straight, gets loss in the bush, can't play cards, can't tell stories, but gets up early. (Wait a minute... I did the cooking!)

Real Tonguer: Term used to describe a useless dog that creates anticipation and excitement for the hunters on their watch during a drive, but that actually aimlessly wanders through the bush barking, baying, and howling, and wouldn't recognize a deer if they came across it.

Foul Weather: Lousy, rotten, miserable, windy, cloudy, damp, rainy, sleety weather. A good day to stay inside.

Fowl Weather: Lousy, rotten, miserable, windy, cloudy, damp, rainy, sleety weather. A perfect day to go duck hunting.

Checked out a new chunk of bush: A substitute for "I got lost." A statement made by a dogger, late getting out to the hunters on the line.

INTRODUCTION

I am a northern Ontario boy who, fortunately, was able to base my working life, and now my retirement, in the north. Well actually, I have turned my hobby into a new career as the "Gun Guy."

I was tagged with the name "The Gun Guy" by one of the politicians during my time as a lobbyist. I am still not sure whether it was derogatory or a term of affection. I am hoping the latter, although I just think he just could never remember my name.

I am an avid hunter of birds, deer, bear, and moose. But it goes without saying, "if you not going to eat it don't shoot it."

I am a proud gun owner, I am a gun collector, I am a recreational shooter, and I am a passionate gun advocate. Guns are an integral part of Canadians' heritage.

I want to ensure that my grandchildren, if they choose to, will be able to continue that heritage.

I have been hunting for over sixty years. It's in my DNA. I am the result of the hunt camp culture, the traditions, the family bonding, the hunting experience, the life experiences, the stories, and the comradeship. Did I mention the stories? This column will give me the chance to share some of those stories with you, and remind you once in a while that we—but I really mean you—have to protect our firearms heritage and way of life.

Growing up, my Grandfather guided deer hunters. For two weeks, our home turned into the deer camp, and the hunters boarded at our house.

For safety and, I imagine, warmth, one of the deer hunters wore a red Santa Claus suit. Even at six or seven years old, I had no problem with it.

The irony of that didn't strike me till later in life.

My long-suffering wife maintains that, at our house, there are only two seasons in the year.

"Hunting season, and getting ready for hunting season"

I am fortunate that my two boys and my 10-year-old granddaughter share this hunting passion. A new grandson arrived this summer, he's been to the hunt camp already, and I am eyeing up hunter orange in his size.

I always prided myself on my ability to juggle and enjoy a number of careers simultaneously. A 35-year career in sales, an adult educator for a Community college, political consulting, guiding, outfitting, timber buyer, and volunteer fireman, to name a few. Who knew… it was only my ADD—Attention Deficit Disorder—in full bloom?

In a past life as CEO and registered political lobbyist for the Canadian Firearms institute, an advocacy and resource group for Canadian firearms owners, I travelled across the country attending over 35 Sports Shows and Gun Shows a year, meeting and talking with firearms owners and hunters. I have enjoyed hundreds of hunting stories. They all have one common thread… they begin with this phrase: "My friend, my father, son, brother, sister (substitute any family member) and I…"

I look forward to sharing some of these stories with you, and expressing my views "From The Hunt Camp Porch."

CHAPTER 1

His story and I am stickin' to it!

At a recent family reunion slash hunt camp meeting, the hunters were standing around having a beverage. In boredom, the non-hunters had drifted off to other areas. As always with our family and friends, the discussion turned to hunting and talk about the upcoming hunting seasons. The meeting was called to order. The first order of business was to whine and complain about the MNRF's (Ministry of Natural Resources and Forestry) lottery system for the tag draw for antlerless deer, and bull or cow moose, and the lack of adult tags for curtain WMUs (Wildlife Management Units), reminding each other and to check and make sure everyone had applied for the appropriate tags in the designated WMUs for the moose draw, and to make sure we got our applications in before the end of June for the deer draws. We hunt in four different WMUs. Are you ready for this? Wait for it! We hold our own family draw to see who applies for a cow, bull, antlerless deer, and in what wildlife unit.

We were commenting on the health and abundance of the local deer population, and game in general, the increased success rate, and how much hunting had improved over the years, but had waned over the last couple of years because of the severe winters.

Then the conversation changed to sharing stories of last fall's hunt, and other past hunts. Seems everyone had a story or two, each one of us trying to outdo the others' stories. That six-point, 130 lb deer that was lying on the ground last fall had matured over the winter, and in the telling was now 8 points, and the shooter swore it was 200 lb, if it was an ounce.

Someone piped up, "the hunting is still not as good as it was in your grandfather's' day." His story had us all beat. We all shared a smile.

I want to share with you this Hunting Story. It's a story my grandfather told in his later years to just about anyone who would listen. I had forgotten all about it.

Now, like all good hunting stories, I am sure there was no exaggeration or embellishment involved.

The story was almost a ritual at the hunt camp or at family gatherings. The memories came flooding back to me.

My grandfather would methodically take out his tobacco pouch, stuff his pipe, strike a wooden match on the seat of his wool mackinaw pants, and slowly and deliberately light his pipe; he would take a few puffs, with the smoke billowing around him, stare at the embers in the bowl, and then settle into his favourite chair and begin.

"Boys… let me tell ya… game was plentiful in those days. We didn't have no hunting season. We hunted to keep the table full; we depended on the meat to survive the winter. I mind the time… I was just a young gaffer, wouldn't a bin more than 13 or 14 years old." Another cloud of smoke from the pipe and he would continue.

"It was late in the fall…a couple of inches of fresh snow…cold as the devil. I was wearing Dad's heavy red plaid mackinaw coat with the big pockets. Dad was off setting up the winter logging camp. We hadn't got any of our winter's meat yet. Mom had sent me out with the old double barrel 12 gauge…that thing kicked like a mule… it did…never liked that gun…used to keep buckshot in one side and bird shot in the other…that way you were ready for anything…"

A few more quick puffs of his pipe and another billowing cloud of smoke. "I was wading across the little crick down behind the barn, at the edge of the bottom 20-acre pasture field on the old homestead...just started to come up the far bank...let me tell you it was as slippery as all get out...had my head down watchin' my footin' when I heard a snap! "A long pause for emphasis, a couple of more draws on the pipe and another cloud of smoke, and he would start again.

"Sure enough...not 10 yards up the hill was standin' the biggest ten-point buck I ever did lay eyes on...I let go with the buckshot...the gun knocked me flat on my ass...back into the water...as I was falling back...the gun pointing up in the air, I accidentally pulled the trigger on the birdshot. I flailed around in the water, that old coat was as heavy as anything when it got wet...I thought I was gonna drown."

A couple of more puffs of his pipe and another cloud of smoke, and he went on. "Well sir...let me tell you...I got myself out of that water and scrambled up the hill...sure enough that buck was layin' there stone cold...to top it off, not ten feet away were layin' two partridge I had knocked out of a tree when I was fallin' back and let go with the birdshot...I reached into my coat pocket to get my cleanin' knife and the pocket was full of speckles..."

He would glance around the room with the straightest poker face you have ever seen. He continued, "You'll not see the likes of that again...Yes sir...without a word of a lie...wasn't gone half an hour...had speckles for the next day's breakfast, partridge for a stew and venison for the larder."

That's his story, and I am stickin' to it!

CHAPTER 2

Best laid plans

The 2016 hunt is over.

Where did the deer go? Should we be worried? I can't remember such a poor harvest or so few sightings since the mid-60s.

I want to talk about the poor harvest this year, but first I have to tell you a story.

Did you hear about the old guy and his two boys who thought they would change things up this year? With the overlapping seasons, they planned to have a nice quiet three-day simultaneous bow hunt for deer, moose and bear… with emphasis on the bear.

The pre-hunt planning, preparations, and scouting had been extensive and ongoing for nearly three months. The game cameras regularly showed three different bears, very few deer, assorted creatures and a moose. Expectations were high. The plan was set.

The two boys utilized tree stands. The old guy has short beagle legs and hunts out of a ground blind. The location of the stands had been well-planned, and had been set up well in advance.

The first morning of the hunt, everyone was in their respective stands bright and early. The plan was to stay there all day. Actually, the plan was to get a bear.

The day turned unseasonably warm with not a whisper of wind. The bush was exceptionally still. It was one of those days; most hunters will recognize it, when even the chipmunks and birds were quiet. You could hear a falling leaf hit the ground.

After a short discussion on the radios, a little disappointed and dejected, they decided to change the plan. They took their lunch kits, and went back to the camp for a mid-day break, with the intention of returning to the bush at about three in the afternoon.

They sat in their T-shirts, grumbled about the lack of activity, and had their lunch at the picnic table by the sliding patio door on the hunt camp porch. After lunch, it was decided that a siesta was in order.

The screen was pulled shut and the door was left open to take advantage of the warm weather. They retired to their respective couches and chair. The old guy, in a chair not far from the door, was stirred by a sound on the deck. He just assumed that it was the boys, up and about. He came fully awake to the bellow of **"Holy!!!!!!! What is that? It's a bear!"**

Sure enough, there was Yogi the Bear, his head stuck in a blue gluten-free soft lunch kit, turning circles like a dog chasing his tail, banging up against the screen door, pawing at his head, trying to get the lunch kit off.

Looking like an old video of the Keystone cops falling all over each other they reached the door at the same time yelling and kicking, trying to shoo Yogi away. Yogi decided he was out numbered and lumbered off toward the bush, lunch kit still on his head.

The adrenalin rush was replaced by hysterical laughter from all, as one of the boys, who had—in his sock feet—chased Yogi to get his lunch kit back, came to a halt at the bush line and picked it up.

I don't think that's how things were planned.

Again, where did the deer go? I am not normally an alarmist but, "Houston, I think we have a problem."

Based on the declining numbers and our experience last year, most of our hunters didn't apply for the antlerless tags and decided to go bucks only. But it seems that wasn't necessary.

From personal experience, the 2016 deer season was a bust. The three different gangs I hunt with, in three different wildlife units, only got one deer over the two weeks. There have been unproductive years in the past. What was alarming about this year was we only saw two deer.

I talked with an outfitter. He runs a commercial operation in the prime deer area and has always had an above average success rate. He accommodates over forty hunters for each week of the two-week season. They only harvested one deer the first week and three the second.

With the exception of a few isolated areas, this scenario was repeated over and over.

I heard a story about an abattoir that specialized in wild game. He butchered over 200 deer in 2014, just over a 100 in 2015, to fewer than 20 this year.

I realize we are on the fringe of prime deer habitat and their population numbers can and do fluctuate. That's normal.

I don't think this dramatic decline is normal. Hopefully when the numbers come in from the hunters' surveys, I will be proven wrong, but I don't think so.

My concern prompted a call to the MNRF and a discussion with a Regional Wildlife Specialist.

He was hearing stories of reduced harvest as well, and was anxiously awaiting the hard numbers.

We discussed and acknowledged that the severe winter and heavy snows of 2014-15 had a devastating effect on the deer herd across the north of their range; as hunters, we noticed the impact last year.

In certain areas, the winter of 2015-16 was bad as well.

Did changing weather patterns affect the hunt? Is it predation? The jury is still out; let's see what the numbers have to say.

THAT DOG DON'T HUNT

CHAPTER 3

Then and Now

Sitting around the deer camp dinner table, I was bragging that I had bought my hunting license online the Sunday before deer season. I have made procrastination a life science. Apparently, I started early. I told the story of getting my first hunting license, again on the Sunday before deer season. A new hunter's course had become mandatory in 1960. Experienced hunters were grandfathered. I considered myself experienced; I had been hunting since I was eight years old.

I was going to school in Toronto and I had stopped into a few sports stores to buy a license, but I was laughed at; none would issue me a license without taking the course.

I was already one year over the age that a license was needed.

Home in the north on the Sunday, I drove into the next town and found the local game warden. I explained my situation and pleaded that I needed a license.

"I have known your grandfather for years and if he taught you how to hunt, you will know more than any course will teach you. I'll bend the rules just once and give you a license."

Now, with that license came one of the biggest blunders ever made by the MNRF at that time; it was called the **Department of Lands and Forest**, a 4" X 12" piece of white paper with your license number on it, a tag bag, and a kilt pin. Your number was to be pinned to your back. Every hunter was a target. It was pre-hunter orange and the white paper looked a lot like the white flash of a deer's tail. The next year they switched to yellow. They only used them for a couple of years.

This recollection was caused by a news item that popped up on my screen when I applied for my license. After 74 years, the state of Wisconsin has quit using the back tags.

I continued to reminisce about the changes to the hunt over the years, and compared them to the present. A few eyes glazed over; I am sure I heard moans and groans, and there was a comment from one of the boys, "*Let me get another beverage; this may take a while,*" but undaunted, I continued.

Times have changed. Yes, they have. The most obvious change is how I went from being the youngest at the camp to now the oldest. Don't know how that happened or why it seemed to happen so quickly.

I began my comparison of then and now.

Then:
The excursion to the moose camp, although within 50 kms of home, was a major undertaking. Travel time was two hours. A rough 4X4 was needed to traverse the last two kms. Outside contact with the world came to an end. Except for a 9-volt battery transistor radio that, after nine o'clock at night was clear as a bell if you were listening to a radio station out of Fort Wayne Indiana, a thousand miles away, an old surplus WWII diesel generator ran for an hour in the morning and evening. The noise could be heard over two townships. The rest of the time, it was propane lights and the wood stove. You carried your water up from the lake. The outhouse was at the bush line.

Now:
You can get a sports car in to the camp and the trip is made in under 35 minutes. A quiet generator runs 24 hours a day. The satellite dish is working and the 50-inch flat screen TV is blaring, somebody is

watching hunting shows, the lights are on, and you turn on the tap to get water, and you flush a toilet.

Then:
We got the weather by looking out the window. Communications in the bush was three shots fired ten seconds apart. You carried a compass and a hand-drawn map. You walked to wherever you wanted to be and carried everything with you. You had no contact with the other hunters other than meeting up for lunch at a pre-arranged spot.

Now:
Cell phones give you an up to the minute weather report. *"It's going to quit raining at 10:34."* If something of interest happens on your watch, a picture is snapped and texted. Everyone texts back and forth; they have a Google map app that shows them where they are, and where the other hunters are. If you need something you hop on the ATV and go back to camp to get it.

Then:
Hunting attire was a red wool plaid jacket, Mackinaw pants, and green un-insulated rubber boots, and usually some type of Elmer Fudd wool hat. Nothing was water proof but your skin. Wool was great as long as you were moving or the wind wasn't blowing. You stood on your watch, suffered, and shivered from the cold.

Now:
Everyone is dressed in expensive, branded, scent free, moisture wicking, waterproof, insulated camo and then we ironically cover that with Hunter Orange… but you are dry and warm.

Then:
Before sunrise, you walked single file through the bush following a red ribbon trail to get to our stands. We looked like the seven dwarfs singing "HI HO HI HO, it's off to work we go." We inevitably never came out were we wanted to be. You can't see red ribbon in the dark.

Now:

THAT DOG DON'T HUNT

At a civilized hour, after a leisurely breakfast and a second cup of coffee, you hop on the ATV and take a groomed trail to your stand, which is marked on the app on your cell.

Then:
If you harvested a moose, it would have to be quartered and packed out on your back or on jury-rigged pole travois, or in the case of a deer, dragged out by three or four of the gang. Through the dense bush; sometimes taking two days. To hang it up on the game pole, an old-fashioned rope block and tackle, and a lot of sweat was needed.

Now:
The ATV does all the work. Secure the head to the back of the machine, and away you go! Drag it easily back to camp and the winch on the ATV effortlessly raises the animal up the game pole.

The changes have been for the better.

What hasn't changed? The good stuff; the comradeship, the hunt camp culture, the hunting experience, the life experiences, the traditions, the family bonding, the stories… did I mention the stories?

CHAPTER 4

It's okay to be a woman hunter!

Just after hunting season, my wife brought to my attention what she thought was an extraordinary number of Facebook postings showing the beaming faces of young girls and women showing off their harvests, or proudly posing with their hunting buddies.

We have a history of female hunters in our circle of friends and relatives and just take it for granted that women are part of the hunting culture. I knew there was an increase in numbers, but… I decided I should investigate! I was enjoyably surprised by my findings.

The American stats indicate that women hunters have increased by 36% in the last number of years and the number of men hunting has decreased by 6%.

Canadian women won't be outdone; the trend is even stronger in Canada. The number of women hunters in Ontario increased by 70%, Alberta almost doubled while B.C. increased by 62%.

Recently three Canadian women reached the semi-finals of *Extreme Huntress*, a TV competition for women around the world. WOW!!!!!!!

Extensive research, including on the Internet, newspaper and magazine articles, conversations with veteran female hunters, frontline professionals, and those new to the sport was an eye opener. The numbers were so strong, and reasons so varied and unexpected.

I queried a couple of the female hunters from my generation as to why and how they started hunting. One stated, *"I started hunting with my dad. I loved being in the bush. I got my license when I turned 15."* She continued, *"When I got married, my husband joined the family hunt camp; now both my daughter and granddaughter hunt."*

The second said, *"I lived-in south-western Ontario and started hunting with my ex-husband. I loved the adventure and the outdoors. It was something we could do together. Now living in northern Ontario, I have been fortunate to be able to continue to enjoy the sport."*

I expected those answers; it's all the reasons that attract men—being with family, the adventure, the love of nature, fun, exercise—all that stuff.

What came next really surprised me.

With the first Internet searches, I found the trend.

STRONG GROWTH IN FEMALE HUNTING AND SHOOTING

MORE WOMEN OWNING GUNS, GOING TARGET SHOOTING AND HUNTING

NUMBER OF WOMEN HUNTERS SKYROCKETS WITH WAVE OF PUBLICITY

I contacted front-liner Bernie Lacasse, a long-time friend, and a firearms and hunting instructor in North Bay, to get his insight.

"Yes, locally it's been a dramatic increase. When I started Hunter Safety in the mid-eighties, women students were around 5%. Now they are about 20-25% of every class."

"I instructed a Canadian Firearms Institute-sponsored Pink Pal Weekend, a full class of ten women taking the Canadian Firearms Safety Course (CFSC). A number of that group went on take the CRFSC (Hand Gun course). One of those girls became a very successful international competitive shooter."

So, ladies, if you are interested in becoming a hunter, it is time to take action. Check out the RCMP website and find an instructor near you. (Firearms safety | Royal Canadian Mounted Police – rcmp-grc.gc.ca). The CFSC (gun course) is ten hours long: the cost, including the book and the exam, is $171.00. The Hunter Safety course offered by your provincial Ministry of Natural Resources is usually about 12.5 hours long: the cost of the course, book, and examination is $185.00. Your license fees are in addition to that.

The other front-liner I contacted was Manitouwadge native and colleague Amanda Lynn Mayhew (www.amandalynnmayhew.com) from Cabalas Pro Staff, Women of the Outdoors, and now the host of her own show "Just Hunt" on WILD TV.

She relayed her experiences: "Raised in the north, gender was never an issue. Moving to Southern Ontario and working in a gun store, I noticed women were not common visitors. When word got out that a female hunter worked in the store, the ladies started piling in and asking questions. Where do I start? How do I start?"

"The number of women in the sport is visibly increasing each year. The rise of social media showcasing women and youths hunting and shooting is growing the sport as never before. It's starting to snowball."

From the articles and the research I pored over, the scholars and experts cited a number of various theories and explanations for the dramatic increase.

I read an article about a group of thirty-something urban Toronto girls. They consider themselves foodies, and had taken to hunting as a means of ensuring organic sources, freshness, and the quality of the meat they used.

With more women involved, manufacturers and marketers are out in front. "It has become a cycle. The more women hunters, the more products they develop, and the more they develop, the more it attracts women," said one expert.

The manufacturers are revolutionizing the sport. Their websites have women-only sections. They are hiring female pro staff. They are producing guns, bows, equipment, and clothing that are designed ergonomically for women. This includes reduced recoil systems, shorter butt stocks, lighter weight materials, shorter lengths of pull-on pump shot guns, etc.

Researchers have weighed in with other ideas contributing to the increase: Women playing less of a domestic role, getting married later, having children later, better-paying jobs and more disposable income, movies like *The Hunger Games*, *The Hobbit*, and *Brave*, which feature skilled female hunters.

I talked with a first-time hunter who joined her uncle's gang. She fell into the above categories. Late twenties, professional, and she came equipped with all the gear—new gun, new clothes. *"It was such a great experience! I want to come back next year,"* she said.

The other novice I interviewed just batted her eyes, and said, "Oh Grandpa (big sigh), I just enjoy being with you." She continued, "You can't beat the excitement of stalking the animals, the fun of watching uncle Jay miss a deer, not to mention getting the time off school."

Whatever the reason, it's great. And it creates a positive perception of hunters.

Let's finish up with these words from Amanda Lynn Mayhew:

"Women have realized it's okay to be a woman hunter. It's okay to shoot a gun or a bow. It's okay to go out there and get your supper on your own, to clean it, process it, and cook it. It's okay to be a woman of the outdoors."

CHAPTER 5

No Skill Needed

I am not a trophy hunter and I have never pretended to be one. My grandfather used to say. "Don't pass on a deer on Monday morning that you would shoot Saturday afternoon. Meat is meat."

But I have got a couple of trophies—known to all that will listen as the "Big Bull" and the "Big Buck."

At a recent family function, we were sitting around having a beverage, and I was about to start telling the story of my "Big Bull" to some unfortunate cousin (a non-hunter) who hadn't heard the story yet, and probably didn't want to hear it.

In an effort to distract me, one of the boys piped up *"Didn't you shoot your "big buck" in the same spot."*

My big buck and big bull were taken about 100 feet and 25 years away from each other.

"Yes! You are right! I had forgotten about that. I'll tell you that story too."

Groaning, with a hint of exasperation in his voice. "Does anybody want another beverage before he starts? We may be here for a while. Dad, can I get you a chocolate bar?"

I like to think otherwise… but there was absolutely no hunting prowess or skill level involved in either story. But there were chocolate bars.

I was in tremendous pain on both occasions.

I turned to my cousin and started.

"There's a 75-acre triangle of bush that the doggers avoid like the plague. On the east, it's bounded by the lake, and on the north and west by the snowmobile trail. It's a low swampy area with little whaleback rock ridges and every wind in the last 100 years has blown a tree over. You can't see anything; you can hardly walk through it. But that's where the game will be. We call it 'the hole'."

We were moose hunting on the west side of 'the hole'.

The big bull was 10 ft away from me when I shot it. I never heard or saw it till it snorted at me.

This was an exceptional moose for our area, WMU 49.

There were no shovels, but the rack was 58 inches. Yes, that's right—58 inches! It must have weighed in at about 1200 lb."

I continued. "I had hurt my back about a week before the season, and I was in severe pain.

I wasn't going hunting. The boys insisted. Opening morning, they helped me get dressed and put on my boots.

We drive moose similar to a deer hunt. I placed everyone on their watches along the snowmobile trail and took the last, and what should have been the worst, spot at the end of 'the hole'.

The run was over. I could see the hunter orange of the dogger. I unloaded, took the magazine out of the gun, and laid it on the back of the ATV. I grabbed the back of the ATV, bent over, and began to stretch my sore back. I whistled to acknowledge that I had spotted the dogger.

While I stood watch, I had been snacking on miniature Halloween chocolate bars. Looking down at the bar wrappers all around my feet, I was thinking, 'I had better pick those up... but I can't bend over to get them'."

For emphasis, and to show how vulnerable I was, I was demonstrating how I was stretching with my butt stuck out. I continued.

"Earlier I had heard something splashing in the water in 'the hole' behind me. I did a very poor impression of a moose call (but apparently a very effective one), and diligently kept watching behind me.

THAT DOG DON'T HUNT

As I whistled—in that prone position with my rear end stuck out—I heard the grunt, and turned around. The bull was 15 feet away, stepping slowly toward me with his head down—challenging me, shaking his antlers from side to side. Time seemed to be in slow motion. I reached for my gun and reloaded… I waited until it raised its head, and shot!!! He ran towards me. I stepped beside the ATV to let him go by; he went about 30 feet and fell. What an adrenaline rush!

When everyone showed up to get the moose out of the bush I proudly and excitedly re-enacted the event showing where I had been standing and how close things were. I was expecting congratulations. NOT!

Someone pointed to the wrappers on the ground. There was a chorus of laughter; 'You lured him in with chocolates!'"

The big buck was shot in the same location, with a lot of similarities in the circumstances.

I started the big buck story. "It was the end of the week and no deer. In desperation, we decided to hunt 'the hole'.

Three of us dogged through 'the hole,' making as much noise and commotion as possible to scare something out. I was just about finished, and then I tripped over a root and severely twisted my knee. I had to cut a crutch to use to get out to the guys.

It was decided I would stay where I was, and the boys would go back to the trucks for lunch and then send someone with 'big red,' the original Honda 3-wheel ATV, to pick me up.

I was sitting on a stump resting my knee, gun across my lap as the guys headed up the trail; I grabbed a chocolate bar for lunch, just took a bite. I heard a snap. Not 20 feet broadside was the big buck, tiptoeing along, and intently watching the guys walk away.

It was a massive old 8-point swamp buck, in full rut; the neck was as thick as could be, the heaviest deer I had ever seen. It was over 300 lb, dry scored 146 on the Boone & Crocket scale.

I stuck the bar in my mouth, raised the gun, aimed and fired. By this time, it was close enough it could have had powder burns on its hide."

Someone heckled. "We'll have to phone the ministry to see if it's legal to bait game with 'Hershey Cocaine'."

Moral of the story—always take chocolate bars with you.

CHAPTER 6

The Waiting Room

I have come to realize the sole purpose and function of retirement. It's not to be able to enjoy life, it's to give you more time to spend sitting in doctors', dentists', pediatricians', specialists', or any number of health providers' waiting rooms.

The minute you get that gold watch, you become the DD for aged parents, spouses, children, grandchildren, and second cousins twice removed.

Recently, during one of these waiting room sessions, I was sitting there looking through a hunting magazine with a picture of a huge bull moose on the cover. It was the signal for a fellow DD to strike up a conversation about the ever-changing hunting regulations, his frustration with the tag system, and the inability of the MNRF to publicize changes, and how he had, to use the phrase, *"just missed the bullet."*

He told this story. *"Last fall my brother, two of his friends, and I went moose hunting up near Thunder Bay. We have been making this trek for the last 20 years, getting up there for the opening week. One of the guys, Paul, from Toronto, had drawn a bull tag. The rest of us had calf tags.*

After 20 hours plus of driving, just turning onto the logging road and reaching the end of cell service, Paul got a call that there had been a death in the family. He had to return to Toronto immediately. We got him into

Thunder Bay and on a flight. The three of us decided that because of all the preparation and effort that we would stay and hunt calves."

The preparation of the gear for these trips is intense. It's a summer camping trip on steroids. You just don't throw a few things in the truck and head out the door. It's like a space launch. You build in a redundancy factor, and bring two of everything. You have to be self-sufficient and comfortable for that week. You have to be prepared for any weather event. You have to be prepared to look after any game you have harvested. The gear consisted of two trucks, one pulling the RV, and the other with a 29-foot trailer full of all the essentials.

He continued. *"We had a great week! Saw a few bulls and lone cows. Finally, mid-week I came across a cow and calf, stalked them for couple of hours till I was finally able to take a shot at the calf—I missed. (Which turned out be pretty fortunate.)*

I got teased relentlessly for the rest of the week. The guys even cut the tail off my shirt."

"With the hunt at its end, we stopped for gas out on the highway. The attendant asked how the hunt had gone. We shared the story of the missed calf. The attendant gave us that look that northerner's sometime use with people from the south." (Yes! You know that look and why we use it.)

He questioned. *"You do realize… calf season is closed this year for the first two weeks of the season? DUH! NO…. Apparently, we deserved that look."*

Soon there were three or four of us swapping stories and experiences.

One elderly gentleman started with a chuckle in his voice. *"Oh, I have got to tell you this story. My idiot son-in-law went on his first fly-in moose hunt with one of his buddies. Kind of an obnoxious character I am told, but a veteran of fly-in hunts. Anyway, they had applied early and were successful with two bull tags, but it was still a last-minute thing because his buddy was having trouble finding an outfitter."*

The pilot landed on a small lake, dropped them and their gear off at a camping spot. The pilot told them it was an overflow site shared with other outfitters. The buddy said "I think I was here last year."

The pilot gave explicit instructions and a warning. "All the bigger Beavers are booked. I am bringing the smaller Cessna in when I pick you up at the end of the week. I will only be able to take the two of you and one moose out without going over the weight limit. So, remember ONLY one moose."

They hunted all week and nothing. The last morning, they were packing and two huge bulls wandered into camp; his buddy grabs his gun and downs both of them. My son in-law is upset. How are we going to get them out of here? Buddy says. "Don't worry about. I'll take care of it."

They had just finished cleaning them up, and the plane dropped down onto the lake.

The pilot runs the plane up on shore, gets out, and he is furious. I told you guys, only one moose! The buddy and the pilot had a heated discussion: The buddy questioned the pilot's abilities; said the other outfitter took two moose out for him last year on a Cessna; threatened to report him for leaving meat to spoil.

Finally, the pilot relents and reluctantly agrees to take the two moose, all the while cautioning how risky it was.

They strapped the two moose to the floats and took off, just skimming the trees: My son-in-law was scared senseless. Struggling to gain altitude, the pilot headed toward base. Shortly they hit some turbulence and crashed into the bush.

"Dazed and happy to be alive, my son-in-law turns to his buddy *"Any idea where we are?"* The buddy said, *'Yeah, right about where our plane went down last year'.*"

Remember!!
Make sure to check the regs for the area you are going to hunt.

From the Hunting Regulations
In-season regulation changes are available at ontario.ca/hunting. Regulations are subject to change from time to time, and it is the hunter's responsibility to be informed of current regulations.

CHAPTER 7

Its going to slap you on the side of the head

Can you envision the old movie scene? A writer sits, pecking away, and then violently tears the paper out of his typewriter, and the scene pans to a huge pile of crumpled paper on the floor.

If I didn't have a delete button on the computer, that would be me.

It's not writer's block; it's disbelief, rage, anger, and frustration with gun owners, politicians, and the general public.

The cause… hunters, gun owners and "The UN Firearms Protocol." *Firearms Marking Regulations*

If you are a hunter/gun owner and say, "what's that," you are the problem!

It's simple. It's complicated.

The Simple.
The UN Protocol, passed back in 2004, is a misguided attempt to identify and trace military firearms used in conflicts in third world countries, but included all firearms, shotguns, hunting, target, and collectible rifles. Every gun imported into this country will have to have "CA" to designate Canada, and the date engraved on it, along with the original serial number, when it comes into the country. Canada doesn't have a domestic firearm manufacturing base. **99% of our hunting guns are imported.**

On the surface it is a warm, fuzzy, feel-good thing that appeals to a certain political bend. It doesn't seem that bad—we are going to save the world from those nasty gun runners. The Canadian government of the time, in keeping with their anti-firearms agenda, hastily signed the protocol, not realizing the damaging consequences. The five largest arms-producing countries didn't sign on, nullifying the effectiveness of the protocol.

My outrage started again in early June at a gun show. Bill Rance, the treasurer of the NFA (National Firearms Association) and I were discussing our amazement that the Liberal Government had postponed the "coming into effect" of the protocol. Some idiot came up to us, and said that we had wasted our money and time over the years fighting its implementation. It was not important.

All gun organizations have worked hard over the years to make this go away, despite the fact that we have—disappointingly—been unable to get you, the hunter/gun owner, concerned and involved.

As retired CEO of the Canadian firearms Institute and for a time the only federally registered political lobbyist for gun owners, it's not my responsibility anymore, and I shouldn't be this upset. But I am!

I can't seem to go a sentence without using a swear word, and then I have to start over.

I want to go on a rant and tell that individual how stupid he is, but it's not my nature. It's taken me a week over my deadline to get this far. (Frank, thank you for your patience.)

Before I talk about the complicated, I am going to take a blood pressure pill and tell you a story.

"A bear just ran in front of me and is heading down in the gully between the two trails," yelled the Youngster.

We had just finish hunting for the day, walking back to camp. The mind of the "Old-timer" was preoccupied; he was tired and anxious to get back to camp. They were losing daylight, about two inches of wet thick snow covered the ground and clung to the bending trees, and the Youngster was walking along a trail on one ridge, while the "Old-timer" was walking along the other ridge.

The gully between them was a thick snow-covered quagmire of storm blown white spruce and hemlock.

The Old-timer could hear the brush snapping as the bear headed straight for him, then suddenly, dead quiet, the bear had stopped.

"You follow the tracks in from your side and I'll go in from this side to the area the noise last came from," yelled the old-timer.

They met up in the densest part, both bent over, heads down trying to keep the snow on the laden boughs, from going down the back of their necks, intent on watching the tracks.

The tracks came up to a den, circled the den, and then disappeared. They were puzzled! No tracks! No bear!

No sign of anything going into the den! What a mystery!

As darkness overcame them, they continued, hunched over, to circle in an ever-widening pattern to see if they could pick up the tracks, but nothing. It was time to go back to camp.

As we started the usual gourmet evening meal, the youngster was asked, *"What were you guys yelling about?"* He immediately started to tell the story.

As he began, the light bulb in their heads came on, as both the youngster and the old-timer, at the same time, realized what had happened: Yogi the Bear had gone up a tree.

Sure, enough we went back at daylight and the claw marks were evident up through the spruce bows on a black ash. Just high enough that if the Youngster had stood up, Yogi could have reached down and parted his hair with his paw.

A life lesson learned! They had been so intent looking down, concentrating on the tracks, intently focused on the den with anticipation, that they ignored the obvious.

I tell you that story so I can make this comment. As gun owners, we can no longer keep our heads down, ignoring the obvious. **The bear (UN Protocol) is going reach down and slap you on the side of the head.**

The Complicated.
The Liberal Government signed the UN agreement back in 2004. The Harper Government, out of principle and to appease the firearms community, annually postponed its implementation, with the last coming into effect of June 1, 2017.

The Liberals have now postponed it until December 2020. Their reason was to allow time to put a bureaucracy in place to administer it... You have time to be heard.

Other than Savage manufacturing 22 and 17 calibre rifles in Canada, all our guns are imported through distributors. Canada, at less than 3% of the global market, is insignificant. At one point, the major manufacturers said they would just walk away from the Canadian market, stop importing guns and selling guns, as well all the branded accessories, shells, hunting clothing, camping equipment, etc.

Goodbye Cabalas... Goodbye Bass Pro... Goodbye Sail... and Goodbye to our local sporting stores.

Hunting contributes just under SIX Billion Dollars yearly to our economy... No Guns available... no hunting.

WHAT THE PROTOCOL IS NOT GOING TO DO:
1. Make our streets any safer.
2. Make it easier to track weapons than it is with what is now available.

WHAT IT IS GOING TO DO:
1. Add a layer of expensive government rules, regulation, and bureaucracy to buying a gun
2. (Best case scenario) Add a significant cost to that gun (estimates are $200-$300 per gun).
3. Stop the importation of guns into the country.
4. Destroy our tourist-based economy.

It's time to stand up, look up and do something.

Contact your MP: Say Thank you for postponing the Protocol, and then let him know why it is important that it not come into effect.

I don't want to hear any whimpering and whining, "I am only one person, I can't make a difference."

You Can!!!

Update: The original article was written in June 2017. As of December 1, 2020, Public Safety Canada announced it will defer the UN marking regulations, which were meant to take effect on Dec. 1, 2020 until Dec. 1, 2023. Its still going to slap you on the side of the head.

CHAPTER 8

My to-do list!

The last column was a rant about the dangers of the UN Marking Regulations. Still, nobody is listening. I didn't get any calls saying someone has to do something.

This column will be a ramble as I think of topics and things to discuss in future articles. My deadline is fast approaching, and I have nothing on paper. This will become my to-do list!

I have procrastination down to an art, but I was always proud of the fact, and thought I was a great multi-tasker… I always had three or four projects on the go, was always extremely active in a number of organizations, and always had a couple of different careers running simultaneously. Turns out, it's not so… I just suffer from Attention Deficit Disorder (ADD) and have a hard time staying with one task. Now as a senior, to compound things, I forget what I am doing, or was going to do, and am prone to repeating tasks—someone is always yelling "Squirrel!"

There you go… speaking of squirrel, I could do a series on hunt camp nicknames, and how they are earned and change with time and events. I have had few over the years. Mine first nickname was "Beagle." Yes, people do tend to look like the pets they own. For a while, I was referred to as "Click;" you can figure that one out on your own. Now, it's "Squirrel."

One guy is stuck with "Veggie," short for vegetarian. The word "vegetarian," I am told, is derived from an old Ojibwa word meaning lousy/ poor/ bad/ hunter.

There you go… I am going to do a couple of articles on successful hunting techniques. Deer, moose, turkey, ducks, caribou—I am good for six or seven months.

This is getting exciting.

I am taking a break and going for breakfast.

Eating breakfast, I was reminded of a conversation, a couple of years back, with a fellow exhibitor at a sports show in Halifax. If you have ever worked a trade show, you realize how important breakfast is. Most shows go on till 9 pm, and you seldom get time for lunch or supper, so you tend to eat a power breakfast. Anyway, a bunch of us met for breakfast. One of the exhibitors, a "fisherman," believe it or not, was an avid anti-hunter. He ate three embryos of a chicken, and a double order of the belly fat of a pig, while expounding on the cruelty of hunting. I just shook my head.

There you go… another series of articles on why we hunt—the need/ the ethics/ the morals of hunting.

Speaking of fisherman…

My apologies to fellow contributor Dan Colomby from Fishing Guide Services or any others.

I have been told that fishermen cannot be believed; they are just plain outright liars.

If a fisherman tells you he caught a ten pounder, you know he is lying, it was only two lbs.

If I have my khaki floppy fishing hat on, you should be a little sceptical of any fishing stories that I tell.

Hunters on the other hand, as part of the culture, after returning to the cave from a successful hunt and the resulting feast, were required as entertainment, and in celebration of the successful hunt to tell of their bravery, skills, and expertise. In the telling of these stories, they were expected and allowed to embellish their exploits; it was quite acceptable. From that time on, that tradition of storytelling has survived.

If I am wearing my hunter orange hat, then you know what I tell you is the gospel. The names, circumstances, location, facts. etc. may be altered to protect the innocent. But it will be based on somebody's reality.

If a hunter tells you he got a ten pointer, you know he got a deer.

Speaking of stories…

This is not a hunting story, but a hunt camp story. Darn near ended in a divorce.

One of my buddies, along with his wife and mother-in-law, were staying at his camp. It's comfortable but rustic; the facilities are outside. To accommodate night visits and to add a level of comfort on the path out to the outhouse he installed a series of the brightest and whitest solar and battery-operated LCD lights. When they are turned on it looks like that supposed white light leading to heaven.

His wife woke him in the middle of the night to a ruckus outside. The outhouse lights were on and his mother-in law could be heard yelling and screaming.

They rushed out to discover the mother-in-law halfway down the path, standing in a halo of light yelling, screaming, and threateningly waving her arms at a huge bear; it was sitting on its haunches with its paws down, by the outhouse door. The wife was screaming at her husband. *"Do something! Do something! What are we going to do?"*

"Nothing," Buddy replied, "The bear got himself into this fight with your mother, let him get himself out of it."

Speaking of bears…

I can do an article on bear behaviour and bear body language.

There you go… I am good for material for articles for a year. Just have to get myself to sit down at the computer and get it done.

JIM NEWMAN

CHAPTER 9

The great Saskatchewan gopher hunt of the summer of 1965

My last article gave me a template for future articles and I was going to stick to it. I was at my computer with all my background material, a few paragraphs into an article on bear behaviour, when one of my Saskatchewan cousins phoned. He wanted to know when I was coming out for a visit and to hunt.

He yelled Squirrel, Ground squirrel, Gopher! So much for bear behaviour.

He reminded me of what became known in the family as *"The great Saskatchewan gopher hunt of the summer of 1965."* So, I have to tell you the story.

My main job for that summer was to stand on a stone boat at the dumb end of a hay baler and manhandle over 7000 fifty-pound straw bales. We built a pyramid of six bales on the stone boat; then stabbed a five-foot iron pry bar into the ground through a trough in the bottom of the boat and let the forward motion of the tractor push them off the boat. You would later go back with the tractor and hay wagon. Load them on with a pitch fork and take them back into the yard.

My other job, the one that created lifelong memories, and which I took very seriously, was to reduce the gopher population. *"Trap or shoot them to near extinction!"* instructed my Uncle. That spring, his prize bull had injured its leg in a gopher hole. He had a hate on for gopher, and I was getting paid a bounty per gopher. Life was good.

With an old Cooey Model 39 single shot 22 and snare wire, I set about it with a passion. Truth be known, I would have gladly paid my uncle.

Although I was not old enough for a driver's license, I drove an un-plated ½ ton truck, older than I was, around the farm for work and on the gopher hunt. I would lay in wait in the box of the truck near a *"gopher town,"* waiting for one to stick its head out of a hole. I swear they could feel the vibration if you were lying on the ground and moved.

On occasion I would sneak into town with the truck, and make a quick stop at the general store to pick up more shells.

My grandfather's mantra, *"Don't shoot anything you are not going to eat,"* kept echoing in my psyche. Why not! As a child of the 50s, I was raised on Daniel Boone and Davey Crocket stories about their expertise with squirrel guns and hunting. They ate squirrels. Gophers look like squirrels. Why can't I eat gophers?

I raised the subject with my Aunt. "If I skinned a gopher and cleaned it up, would you cook it for me?"

"Sure" she said. "You bring one in cleaned up, I'll cook it."

Coffee break for the men was in the kitchen at ten o'clock every morning, and we were expected to be out of house promptly.

For the women, coffee break was at 10:30.

Telephone party lines were still the norm, and religiously, at 10:30 every morning, my aunt and eight neighbours on the party line would pick up their phones and chat, get crop and weather reports, gossip, visit, exchange recipes, and basically just assure each other that there were other people in the world.

Keep in mind that these neighbours were miles apart.

I never knew this story until her passing; it was mentioned in her eulogy. She had said yes to cooking the gopher, not thinking

THAT DOG DON'T HUNT

I would do it. When I did show up with the cleaned gopher, she was frantically on the party line soliciting everyone's help to make sure gophers were safe to eat. The party line was frantic, a special afternoon session called. Anyone who owned an encyclopaedia was tasked with research, and one even phoned the Vet.

The women of the group started to refer to me as *"that crazy eastern kid,"* and that name lasted for a number of subsequent visits over the years.

As the summer progressed, able to observe and understand gopher behaviour, and as my shooting skills improved, my success rate increased to the point where my uncle wanted to renegotiate the bounty system. Actually, what he said was, *"I don't hate gophers as much as I thought now that it's costing me money."*

"Gopher bounties… you are just like your dad." My aunt first told me the story during that summer, and my father later filled in more of the details.

My father, his two brothers and three sisters were children of the depression. Their mother died in childbirth, the girls were all dropped off at various Aunts, and the boys were left to fend for themselves as their father travelled around to find work.

The boys helped out at a butcher and a bakery shop for food.

At that time the townships offered a one cent per tail bounty on gophers, and that was the boys' source of income. They were professional hunters so to speak. LOL

My aunt explained. "The Newman homestead was on the boundary of two townships. It was four miles into either town. Weekly the two youngest boys would take the tails into the township office to collect the one cent bounty. The oldest one would wait around the side of the building. The clerk would count the tails, and because they stank so badly, he immediately took them out to the back of the building, and then come in and pay the boys the bounty. The oldest would re-acquire the tails and the next day they walked the eight miles there and back to the other township office, and collect the bounty there, too."

Dad later admitted that he was sure both clerks knew what the boys were up to, but felt sorry for them and turned a blind eye.

Memories! The great gopher hunt of 65! I kept that gopher hide for years. I finally threw it out a few years back, and that was the first and last time I ever ate a gopher!

CHAPTER 10

Ursus americanus

Bear season just opened, so let's talk about bears.

Up until 1961, there was a bounty on black bears and hunting was unrestricted. Between 1942 and 1961 in Ontario an average of 850 bears a year were turned in for the bounty. A separate bear license was introduced in 1980. From 1961 till then, the bear license was combined with your deer license.

I have always been fascinated by Black Bears and have a tremendous respect for their intelligence, curiosity, cognitive skills, and strength. I have observed and interacted with them in the wild for a lifetime.

I consider myself an expert on Eastern American Black Bears (*Ursus americanus*). I know nothing about Polar Bears, Grizzly Bears, or what I didn't even know existed till I started this article, the Newfoundland Black Bear (*Ursus americanus Hamiltoni*). It has one of the longest hibernation periods of any bear in North America. It's generally bigger than our local bears, and are they are half an hour ahead of them.

Once I get going, and I am not distracted, this will turn into a multi-column project. In this and the next few issues, we will talk about bear facts and then onto bear behaviour and body language after that.

If you are going to declare yourself an expert, then it's imperative to outline your credentials. I don't want anyone out there saying, *"He doesn't know what he is talking about."*

Just to be clear I have no formal or academic background on the subject.

My qualifications:
1. When I was two years old, I got a 24" teddy bear that I carried for years.
2. I have used bear-infested rural municipal dumps for years.
3. I have called the MNR Bear line, not once, but twice.
4. I wake my wife in the middle of the night, screaming at bears in my dreams.

Outside of those qualifications all my comments are based on years of interaction (sometimes a little too close for comfort), observation, voluminous reading, learning from elders and other knowledgeable individuals, and now Internet videos.

American Black Bears are not closely related to Grizzly, Brown or Polar bears; genetic studies reveal that they split from a common ancestor over five million years ago.

The American Black Bear is the world's most common bear species. Not all black bears got the colour memo; some can be brown or tan, and there are reports over the years of non-albino white bears. (They are actually a light tan colour).

According to the MNRF, there about 95,000 bears in Ontario, and they can be found throughout the province, with concentrations in the Algonquin Park area and the Chapleau Crown Game preserve. The population decreases the farther north you go.

Males have a heavily muscled developed neck, shoulders and forearms and a large broad head. If you are looking at a bear and its ears seem too small, it is probably a male. The female is thinner in the shoulders, and has a thinner snout. The ears are more prominent.

Bears live up to 30 years old in the wild. We have a huge, what is now an old, male with a disfigured jaw that has been coming into our village dump for well over 20 years.

Males range from 250 to 600 pounds (114 to 272 kg), females from 100 to 400 pounds (45.4 to 182 kg). Males max out in size about at seven or eight years of age, and females at about five years.

Bears are omnivores, which means they eat plants and berries, and from time to time you might look like a snack. They eat carrion in the spring and are the predominate predators of calf moose. A bear was observed following a cow moose for days waiting for her to drop the calf.

Depending on food supply their body weight can fluctuate dramatically throughout the year and from year to year. When food is plentiful bears can gain 2 to 3 lbs per day. They will sometimes double their weight from spring to fall. If food is scarce... what was 400 lbs last year may be only 300 lbs this year.

Bears do hibernate in covered dens, but most times it is just a nest in a hollow, a crevasse on a side hill, or against a log or wind fall. It was believed that hibernation was the result of colder weather and shortened daylight, but there is more and more evidence that it is based on food supply. As the food sources dry up in the fall, the bear's metabolism changes; it goes into hibernation mode to protect the fat the bear has gained over the summer.

I have had the opportunity to climb into a traditional bear den and observe Yogi fast asleep. I didn't realize at the time, but bears are actually light sleepers and can be wide awake immediately. Years ago, one of our hunters stepped on what he thought was a snow-covered rock. The bear knocked him off his feet as it jumped up and ran off.

It's been observed that Bears stick around their den sites for a couple of weeks after they wake in the spring. My grandfather told me that was because they were groggy. In actual fact, they lose the calluses off the bottom of their paws during hibernation, and it's uncomfortable for them to get around. Sows with cubs will actually pick a den site in the fall that has a large tree nearby, usually a white pine, so that in the spring, cubs can scramble up the tree to get out of danger instead of running away.

If there is an abundance of food, sows usually have cubs every second year. The cubs will stay with the sow for about eighteen months.

Bears mate in June and July. The sows have delayed implantation. If food is scarce and they do not gain a specific amount of body weight through the summer, then the fertile eggs are not implanted in the uterus but absorbed by the body. Genetic research indicates that cubs from the same litter may have different fathers.

I am just getting started and I am out of space…continued next issue. http://www.ontarioblackbears.com/facts.html

CHAPTER 11

More on Black Bears!

Last issue we just started to talk about the bear's love life when I ran out of space, so I have started this issue with an overlap of a couple of paragraphs from last month.

If there is an abundance of food, sows will usually have cubs every second year. Apparently, they will have from one to four cubs, with two to three the norm. The cubs are born in January and will weigh less than a pound. They will stay with the sow for about eighteen months.

Bears mate in June and July and it seems the sows are promiscuous. The sows have delayed implantation. If food is scarce and they do not gain a specific amount of body weight through the summer, the fertile eggs are not implanted in the uterus but absorbed by the body. Genetic research indicates that cubs from the same litter may have different fathers.

The most predominate predator of bears aside from humans is Black Bears. A boar will kill existing cubs so it can mate with the sow and ensure its own genes are passed on.

That is why sows are so protective of their cubs.

I have read of accounts of the sow and boar getting into near fatal battles at mating time; and both having extensive injuries.

Bears are like humans; they can be lazy, and are opportunists. If your barbeque smells like dinner, it will be dinner, and they will keep coming back.

Studies of black bears suggest they have intense senses of smell and hearing.

I haven't seen any studies on their eyesight, but they certainly love to stand on their haunches and look around.

The cartoon character Yogi Bear's claim to fame was that he was *"smarter than the average bear."* If that was so, he must have been brilliant.

Bears are one of the more intelligent animals. New studies and research indicate that bears have phenomenal cognitive skills, sometimes equal to those of apes, and they will use tools. One study showed bears hauling in logs and debris to stand on to get at a suspended bait. They have excellent long-term memory, and unparalleled sense of direction and navigation skills—sort of a built-in GPS.

The average range for a male is 15-30 km. I have been told that in times of scarce local food supplies a GPS tagged bear travelled well over 100 km in a direct line to get to a lush blueberry patch that he had visited several years before.

As a confirmation of their navigational skills, a retired MNRF employee tells the story of trapping a nuisance bear in Wanapitei, east of Sudbury. *"On a Tuesday, it was in the live trap. We sprayed it with a patch of red paint, transported it up Hwy 144, and released it in Halfway Lake Provincial Park, some 200 plus km by road, and 100 km as the crow flies from Wanapitei. We then went on to the Timmins office for the rest of the week. We arrived back in Sudbury mid-afternoon on the Friday just in time to receive a call about another nuisance bear at the same location in Wanapitei. Sure enough... we get out there to reset the live trap, and there was the red painted bear with his head stuck in a garbage can."*

He chuckled and said, "The bear actually beat us home."

NOW, the big question. "ARE BEARS DANGEROUS?" I will attempt to give you the definitive answer... Yes, No, Maybe, Maybe Not, Sometimes, and Sometimes Not...

ALL BEARS HAVE THE POTENTIAL TO BE DANGEROUS!

That's about as clear as I can get… they are always unpredictable. In any bear encounter, you have to assume they are dangerous.

Even bear skin rugs can be dangerous. I have seen people trip over them, fall, and get hurt.

Keep in mind that until 1961 there was a bounty on bears, and if they interacted with humans, it wasn't going to be a positive experience, or it would be their last time. Momma taught the kiddies to stay away from those dangerous crazy humans.

We now have generations of bears that aren't afraid or threatened by humans. By nature, they are very inquisitive animals, and are apt to stand up and take a look at you to determine whether you are a threat or not.

In another time, if you saw a bear in the bush, it was usually a ball of black fur running away from you at 30 mph. If you had a close encounter, it was an accident.

Black bears would make great poker players. They love to bluff. They will try to intimidate you to scare you off.

They will click their teeth, salivate, huff and puff, pound their front paws on the ground, and make a false charge at you. They will repeat this dance, getting closer and closer, until you back off, or they decide you are bigger than they are. If they do determine you as a threat, they usually don't have the intent to hurt you. It's a defensive move on their part, but they will charge you and run you over to get by. Imagine playing football without any equipment on, and getting hit by a 350 lb linebacker running at full speed. Even if he is wearing a big black fur coat, you are going to get hurt.

Unprovoked predator black bear attacks are very rare. A predator bear will likely be a two or three-year-old rogue male. It will have stalked you and approached from behind.

I have an acquaintance who, as a child, was coming up from the shoreline at their camp in northwestern Ontario. The predatory black bear attacked, mauled, and bit him. It took hundreds of stitches to patch him up. He was fortunate not be one of those rare fatalities. I have been told there have been seven fatalities since 1916 when recordkeeping was started.

Check out the MNR Bear Wise website *ontario.ca/bearwise* for all the does and don'ts when it comes to bear encounters.

It seems no one has yelled "Squirrel" yet, and I am not bored with the subject, so next time, more on bears.

CHAPTER 12

How you doin' Mr. Bear?

A lifetime in the bush, hunting and working, has allowed me in the range of thirty up-close and personal encounters with bears in the wild, where I got fleeting opportunities to observe their behaviour and actions.

My first encounter was as a youngster.

I had bicycled out the three or four miles from town to my favourite Speckle stream in a steep gully just off the road. Between the road and the gully was a chest high thick wall of what my grandfather called Marsh Ferns.

Returning to my bike after a successful fish, fighting my way through a particularly thick patch of marsh ferns, I looked like the Karate Kid doing the praying mantis pose. I was tiptoeing along, trying to avoid getting my feet tangled in the stems or getting cut by or snagged on the fern's fronds, holding high my fishing rod in one hand and a Y-shaped alder twig holding my speckles in the other. My eyes were on the reel, trying to avoid getting the line snagged.

I physically walked in to a yearling cub. We both staggered back. It stood up on its haunches to take a look at what it had run into, we were nose to nose. With a squeal it turned and ran off. It left a pile of scat. I don't recall… but my underwear was probably stained as well. As memorable and comical as the incident was, it was over in a flash—it wouldn't have been more than a mere ten seconds. I was hooked on bears.

If you summed up all the time involved in my encounters with bears, it probably wouldn't total more than 30 minutes.

You've got to love YouTube! I just spent over four hours on my computer, safely watching videos of bears. Over and over, they show the classic response to people or threats.

Bear body language 101: Their body language is a good indicator of their intentions.

Black bears love to bluff. They will try to intimidate you to scare you off. They will click their teeth, turn their lips up in a snarl like a dog; they salivate, huff and puff, pound their front paws on the ground, and make a false charge at you. Usually, the louder and noisier a bear is, the less dangerous it is. It is trying to scare you off.

Your reaction to black bears should be counterintuitive. Don't panic. Don't run away. Stand your ground, and make yourself look as big as you can. You have to intimidate them. Start by talking to them in a calm matter, and if that doesn't seem to work, then raise your voice and start yelling and waving your arms. If you have to retreat, keep your eyes on the bear and back up slowly, don't turn your back on them and run. That sends a message to them that you are frightened and more than likely prey.

If a bear is sitting up on its haunches, relaxed, with its head and nose high, and its paws limp in front of it, you are relatively safe. It doesn't feel threatened and is just trying to see what you are and get your scent. On the other hand, if it is standing up with its head and nose straight at you, and you can see the pads of its paws, you have an unhappy bear.

Keep in mind that bears are always unpredictable. You don't know—even they don't know—how they are they are going to react in any given situation.

In my first article on bears, I listed my qualifications, the last of which was:

4) I wake my wife up in the middle of the night screaming at bears in my dreams.

THAT DOG DON'T HUNT

I recall one encounter with a young male that is no doubt the basis for those dreams. I was running a property line on an oak-covered side hill, and had just climbed down a little rock face. I turned around and the bear was about thirty feet in front and to my right with its back to me; its head stuck in a pile of oak leaves, scrounging for acorns. The bear hadn't yet realized I was there. I had a ten-foot rock face to my left, the rock behind me and a rather steep slope to my right. No where to go.

If you read the rule book on the list of things of how to be prepared, and what not to do in a bear encounter, I would be able to scratch most of them off the list. I had broken every cardinal rule.

I didn't have a practical escape route. The bear only had one escape route. I was too close. The bear was eating. The bear didn't know I was there. I was about to startle the bear. No bear spray, no whistle—just a compass and a 100-foot measuring tape.

It seems kind of feeble now, but I remember it clearly. In a calm conversational voice, I said "Hey Mr. Bear, how are you doing?"

The bear immediately turned toward me, stood right up on its hind legs, stretching as far as he could, staring at me with what I assumed was a look of surprise, the pads of its paws pointing directly toward me. It came down clicking its teeth and pounding its paws on the ground, coming closer each time.

My back was literally up against a wall, no place to go. I stretched up waving my arms and the measuring tape in the air, yelling "Go away!" at the bear, in a language I sure he understood.

I stood up on a fallen log to make myself look bigger, still yelling and frantically waving. The bear kept coming, clicking its teeth and pounding its paws on the ground. It got about ten feet away, then stood up on its haunches with its paws down. It turned and slowly sauntered off. Again, as terrifying as it was, that whole encounter couldn't have lasted more than a minute.

I tell you; I'll take the four hours of YouTube anytime.

CHAPTER 13

My sister and I had the best swing in town!

I just recently realized what most of you already knew; I am not the sharpest knife in the drawer. It's taken me 65 years to realize it. A number of things came together this year to bring me to that realization: 1) recalling a hunting season from childhood, 2) my mother moving into a seniors' residence, 3) sitting on a pile of red pine poles, and 4) finding a long-lost picture.

I'll explain a little later.

Another hunting season is in the books. That's a generalized statement to a multi-layered passion. Each of the hunts is unique and has its own challenges. There is bear hunting, partridge hunting, turkey hunting, duck hunting, wolf hunting, deer hunting, and moose hunting, and then you can double that by factoring in the bow hunt.

Physical limitations only allowed me one day of moose and three of deer, but it proved to be one of the most memorable, rewarding, and successful seasons.

Successful: Success was not based on what was hanging on the game pole. It was based on the good times spent with family and friends.

The Saturday before "Deer" has evolved into Family Day at the camp. The hunters, spouses, children, grandparents, and family friends gather for a day of camp chores, ATV'ing, scouting, exploring, feasting on smoked treats (Jerky, cheese, sausages, etc.), a barbeque, and ending with a camp fire. I enjoyed that more than any hunt.

One of the chores was cleaning up and mounting the antlers from last year. Around the camp fire, I recalled, as a youngster, getting our picture taken sitting on the back of a deer holding the antlers. (Now that Mom has moved, boxes of family albums are sitting in my office; I should look for that picture.)

Rewarding: The boys and I try to get a few days to hunt just by ourselves. With my inability to commit to the moose hunt this year, we all ended up in different locations. I received this text as I was settling in for the night.

"Wish you all the best for tomorrow. Though we are not together, we may be kilometres apart, yet are close at heart. We share the same passion and will have the stories to share; they will unite us throughout the year. Please be safe. Cheers and thank you for instilling this season."

Life doesn't get better than that!

Memorable: After years of being the dogger, you develop a method of hunting that suits your opportunities. The shots that I took were reactive and limited to seconds. The deer was a moving target in full flight out of its bed, or it had stayed still and hidden for as long as it could before it bolted. I was using a new open-sighted gun this year, so I practiced and practiced my shooting routine, setting up a number of targets spaced at variable distances apart; rapidly taking two shots at each target. I was on target… the gun was working perfectly.

So, what happens in deer season cannot be blamed on the gun. *"You can't teach old dog new tricks"* is true. Evidently, if I have time to slowly aim, whatever I am shooting at is safe.

I set a personal record of the most shots fired at a standing deer without hitting it!

I had just set up my chair on a pile of red pine logs at the edge of a clear-cut, and sat down to make sure it was stable. It was bush in front and wide open on both sides. To ensure I had optimized my line of sight, I looked left and then turned right… Wow, a little over 100 yards off, a doe stepped out from the edge of the bush. With difficulty I climbed down off my perch, slapped the magazine into the gun, and racked up a shell. The doe busted me and turned back into the bush. I stood there, dejected at a missed opportunity. It popped out again, standing broadside. I slowly took aim and fired; it hopped out further into the clearing and stopped. I fired again—nothing. Still broadside, it hopped, and I fired again, decapitating a field spruce just inches over its back and just behind it. Seven times I fired at it broadside; unphased, it turned and hopped away. My last shot was a F*** You at the tail. Knowing I was out of shells, seemingly unconcerned, it stopped, turned and looked back. I swear it stuck its tongue out at me before walking away.

I use to joke that my method of hunting with the rapid shots was to "lay down a barrage and let the deer run into it." Now I have to joke that my new method is to lay down a barrage and let them walk out of it.

Now, let me explain about the swing.

When I was a youngster, the "deer hunt" was a source of income. Our house was converted to "The Camp." The house was overrun by 10 to 12 paid hunters, and the woodshed stored all their gear. My grandfather and great uncle guided. My sister and I were given chores, and it was long days for my mom and dad, keeping the hunters pampered and fed. The cooking was done on a wood stove. I can still smell the homemade bread and freshly baked pies. I remember sitting at the supper table, enthralled, listening to the hunters' stories.

At one of those suppers my grandfather stated with enthusiasm, "Kids, next spring Uncle Norm and I are going to build you a new swing."

Right after spring thaw, towering peeled red pine poles appeared in the yard. Holes were dug. The top cross beam was scribed and saddled. New sturdy one-inch rope was strung. It was a thing of beauty. We spent our summer on that swing.

THAT DOG DON'T HUNT

Just before I started this column, I found the picture. Sure enough, there with big smiles, were my sister and I in front of our new swing, each sitting on the back of a buck, holding the antlers. In the background are three other deer hanging from the swing.

Now as I looked at the picture, I realized it may have been a swing, but was built as game pole. All these years, I was living a lie.

CHAPTER 14

You may not get the hat

What's in a name?
"That which we call a rose. By any other name would smell as sweet."
I can't believe I'm quoting Shakespeare.

My apologies to my high school English teacher for arguing, *"I don't know why we have to waste our time studying Shakespeare. I'll never use it."*

Depending on the occasion, what camp I am at, or whom I am with, I will answer to Beagle, Jimbo, Click, Squirrel, Hershey, "dinner is ready," and even just a plain old, Hey you!

Studies show that a name influences how people identify you, react to you, how they think of you, how they judge your character.

"A name can also be a self-fulfilling prophecy. If your name sounds intelligent, successful and attractive, you are more likely to act those things," said Richard Wiseman (case in point), the author of one of the studies. He went on to say, *"your name can influence your career. There are a disproportionate number of dentists named Dr Payne."*

Comedian George Carlin used to do a routine about man's needs to form close and inclusive groups, he commented, *"the first thing they do is get funny hats and give each other names like 'Grand Poobaa'."*

Native American natives' names were often chosen to mark major events in life, and could change with new achievements, life experiences, and accomplishments.

THAT DOG DON'T HUNT

All these observations are proven true at hunt camps.

Some people can spend their whole hunting career and not get branded. There is no shame in this. In fact, usually the name is not a badge of honour.

Your nickname has to be earned, usually by doing something stupid or doing something consistently, but truth be known, it's usually both. It can change in a flash or with a new event.

Mine started out as "Beagle." Yes, people do tend to look like the pets they own. With my short legs, I had to walk around things instead of over them like everyone else in the camp.

For a while I was referred to as "Click;" you can figure that one out on your own. Now it's "Squirrel."

One guy is stuck with "veggie," which is short for vegetarian. The word *"vegetarian,"* I am told, is derived from an old Ojibwa word meaning lousy hunter.

Here are a few other names that come to mind. I could fill three or four columns on the details and stories of how people earned their nicknames, but I'll save that for another time.

Compass: He is never sure in which direction he is going or where he has been and has a completely different perspective of a bush than everyone else. He sometimes goes in circles, but he goes.

Hound dog: Steadily on the go, sometimes a little dishevelled. Does all the dogging, and when he gets on a deer track, he stays on it. He has been known to bark like a dog.

Pointer: *"Oh Look! There are two deer,"* he happened to exclaim, as he pointed them out to Hound Dog instead of taking a shot at them.

Miss Kitty: Her given name starts with a "K," and her first shot at a deer was a miss. (I didn't realize "Gunsmoke" was still in reruns. And that it would be recognized by the youngsters).

Tin Cup: He hunts near a golf course and had a deer run at him across one of the greens.

Poo: No... I know what you're thinking! The name is a derivative of "Winnie The Pooh." He shot a very small bear. He answers to either "Winnie" or "Pooh."

I have survived a couple of hat episodes.

Back in the early eighties, to set us apart, we decided we would have some logo hats made up for the members of our moose camp. Considerable time was spent designing the crest for the hats during, "at work," hours, I might add. A name was chosen, "Howard Hilton Hunt Camp," and we even got a consensus of what colour of red to use. (This was pre-Blaze/Hunter orange.) We were happy; it reflected the owner's name, reflected the luxury of our camp, and it rolled nicely off the tongue. We special ordered them, just twelve hats...it was right down to the wire. They were picked up from the "hat guy" on the Sunday on the way into the hunt camp. If memory serves me right, they cost about $20.00 a hat, a lot of money in those days. In anticipation, most of us didn't bring hats. The new hats were handed out with great expectations and fanfare as we sat down to Sunday supper. The hats looked great, there was a lot of excitement, and everyone liked the logo. It was like Christmas.

George piped up, *"Is there a larger size, mine is too small."* *"So is mine,"* chirped someone else. Sure enough, all twelve hats were size small. All but two of us went hatless for the hunt. Mine still hangs unused on a set of antlers in my gun room.

A couple of years back, "The Boys"—the younger generation (smarter than the older generation)—and a number of their friends that they grew up with, formed their own deer camp. I have been fortunate to be included in the camp. As the group solidified, it developed into the *"Gettin' Good"* hunt camp. They had been together long enough, and had made a desperate quest to give each other nicknames. The hat committee spent hours deciding on nicknames for everyone.

The decision was made to order hats in both camo and hunter orange, with the camp name up front and everyone's nicknames across the back. Again, they were all special ordered; a detailed list of the nicknames was provided. Having heard the story of the original hats, they ordered adjustable sizes. Again, they were picked up on the Sunday on the way into camp. Again, they were handed out with fanfare. As they came out of the box, it soon became apparent that the hats all had the same name across the back. Every one in hunter orange and camo was *"Hound Dog."*

You can earn the nickname… but you might not get the hat!

CHAPTER 15

I've got a sore neck!

Since December I have been like one of those bobble neck caricatures... head just a-bobbin'.

I have been shaking my head in dismay at the uproar and backlash, or whatever you want to call it, caused by Steve Ecklund's posting on his Facebook page of his Alberta Cougar hunt, and then using the meat in a stir fry.

Contest, you can win a Cougar cookbook!

You just have to guess... "What has 900 likes, 450 comments, **13 confirmed death threats**, 754 swear words, and pictures of a smiling happy hunter?" If you are having trouble, it's Steve's Facebook page. Check it out, those cougars are huge!

Steve's a Northern Ontario boy now living in Alberta; he is one of the hosts of a hunting show, "The Edge," on Wild TV. According to his bio, hunting is his passion; he was raised in a family of hunters, and the hunting environment. He is an ambassador and a pro staffer for Cabela's. Back in the late fall, he had the opportunity to go on a successful "Northern Alberta lion hunt with BIG CAT ADVENTURES Brian and Claudette Chorney."

Jeff Foxworthy has his own Redneck dictionary... I think here on the Porch we are going to start our own "The Porch" dictionary.

The first word in the book will be "Anti Hunter," pronounced Sanctimonious: (sanc·ti·mo·ni·ous), a derogatory adjective: 1).

making a show of being morally superior to other people, self-righteous, holier-than-thou, pious, pietistic, moralizing, preachy, smug, superior, and hypocritical.

My head is shaking… 13 Death threats! The "antis" don't think we should hunt animals but condone killing humans. Oh, my neck is sore.

This is a very emotional issue, and as with all emotions, sometimes we humans are irrational and put our mouth in motion before starting our brain. I certainly hope that is the case with most of the social media comments, but (head shaking) **13 death threats**…

Further creating a national and international reaction to the Facebook posting, ex-first lady Laureen Harper—known for her love of cats, and sometimes referred to by the Ottawa press as "The Cat Lady"—weighed into the discussion and called Steve a jerk, and made a comment about his penis size.

Shaking my head again… never missing an opportunity, the Conservative Party of Canada, pretending it wasn't one of their own that inflamed the issue, immediately started a social media fundraising campaign letting everyone know they were the only party that would protect hunters and gun owners. Shake, shake, and shake.

Let's look at the facts. Cougars (*Puma concolor couguar*), sometimes called Mountain Lions, Puma, or Panthers, are not endangered in Alberta—far from it—in fact, in some areas they are a threat to livestock and humans. They are a well-managed wildlife resource. A quotas system is used for both male and female animals, with an open season for both residents and non-residents.

According to online sources, the recent annual quota in Alberta allowed up to 155 cougars to be harvested by residents, in season, with another 30 cats allotted to non-residents. There were 1,025 licenses given out in the 2016-17 hunting season and 125 cougars were harvested.

So far this season, which is open until the end of February 2018, no more than 775 licenses have been sold.

The province says there are between 2,000 and 3,500 cougars in Alberta.

The life span of Cougars is about a dozen years; they stand about three feet high (90 cm) at the shoulders—yes, that's right, males weigh in about 220 lb (100 kg) with the females ranging up to 140 lb (64 kg). They are at the top of food chain… Again, my head is shaking in disbelief—you can't convince me that they are going to be frightened of anything. Contrarily to the antis' claims that they are frightened little animals.

Over the last century there have been a number of deadly cougar attacks on humans, the majority against children.

Here are a few of the social media comments both for and against; you are allowed to shake your head, too. I am giving out awards.

Most Canadian-like response:
zeezo69x: "This could've all been avoided if he made his post private, in this day and age of Internet outrage he should've known better than posting dead kills. It's like he wanted to get harassed."

Most Reasoned:
passionforfishing: "All you cow and chicken eaters… your butcher does your dirty work for you because you pay money at the supermarket. It's legal to hunt and the meat is a food source. I'm a city person, too, and NO, I'm not a hunter, but there is nothing wrong with what he did. YES, cougars are beautiful creatures, but we were all once hunters."

Most Unreasoned:
Diane Lalonde: *"You are a sick individual. You should be shot."*

Runners up for most Sanctimonious (Head-shakers):
"Imagine that you are alone free in your environment and natural habitat, searching for food to survive and care for your young. Then a psychopath hunts you, not for survival, but for gratification and predatory satisfaction… This human predator lacks empathy or respect for nature or the beauty and wonder of all species. It's tragic and heart breaking with so many species on the brink of extinction. We are all connected to nature and have a responsibility to protect

animals and their habitat. Be an ambassador of sustainability and hope, not violence."

Further inflaming emotional content and diversifying the discussion, hounds are used in a cougar hunt. Apparently, cats and dogs don't mix. It was head-shaking to read some of the comments from the antis as well as other hunters. It was acceptable to hunt upland birds with cute little spaniels, ducks with a faithful Labrador or other retrievers, rabbits with beagles, or hounds for deer, but not dogs for cats. My head's just a bobbin'.

Shaking my head one last time in dismay and disappointment... This time directly at Steve... If he had a do over, the only thing that I can see that he should have changed was to have invited me to go along on the hunt.

Got to go find some painkillers for this sore neck.

CHAPTER 16

Is it a *gun* problem or a *society* problem?

I am going to weigh in on the discussion of gun control in the US and how it affects gun owners in Canada.

I am more aware of the nuances of gun control in Canada than most people are.

As Chief Executive Officer of the Canadian Firearms Institute, and for a time the only registered federal lobbyist for the gun community, I dealt with the issue on a daily basis. In fact, I was tagged with the name "The Gun Guy" by one of the politicians. I am still not sure whether it was derogatory or a term of affection. I am hoping the latter, although I think he just could never remember my name.

Does Canada need more gun control? Absolutely NOT!

Does the US need more gun control? I don't know. That's up to them.

Talking gun control is like discussing religion or politics. Emotions are front and centre, and common sense and the facts take a back seat. Everyone has an opinion and everyone believes they are absolutely right.

Nearly fifty years ago, the other Trudeau commented about living next to the US. I paraphrase, *"It is like sleeping with an elephant; you are going to feel every twitch and grunt."* **If it rolls over you are going to get squashed.**

Every Canadian can tell you what Trump is doing… but a large percentage of Canadians don't even know or care who our Prime Minister is or what is happening in Ottawa. We are bombarded by CNN, Fox News and the US media. We are more influenced by events in the United States than in our own country.

It is important for Canadians to remember this is Canada, not the US.

Their problems are not our problems.

The US constitution has the 2nd amendment, *"The right to bear arms,"* and it preserves the power of the individual states, giving them control over gun legislation. It is the individual states' domain. Gun control is not one of the powers delegated to Congress, but instead is vested in the states. Each of the states has their own rules and regulations for the purchase, possession, licensing, and carrying of guns.

The only powers available to Congress to regulate firearms are the "commerce powers," arising from the Commerce Clause, and the "taxing power." Congress is constitutionally restricted in what they can legally do. Throw the influence of the National Rifle Association (NRA) into the equation, and Congress is very unlikely to do anything.

In Canada, for good or bad, we have a national firearms law. It's the same from coast to coast to coast.

The concept of an US unregulated, anything goes gun wielding society is a paradox. In fact, the majority of the most populous states, Florida excluded, have far more draconian gun laws than Canada does.

There are more than thirty states that allow licensed or unlicensed, concealed or open carry, permits for hand guns. Some states have no gun laws at all, while others have very restrictive laws.

Back in 1994, in keeping with their "Commerce Clause," the US Congress enacted "The Federal Assault Weapons Ban (AWB)" prohibiting: 1) the manufacture, transfer, and possession of "NEW" semi-automatic assault weapons; and 2) the transfer and possession of large capacity ammunition feeding devices. It could not and did not control any existing guns. The AWB contained a sunset provision declaring that it would expire ten years from enactment. Congress allowed the ban to expire on September 13, 2004.

Just after the last school shooting. Kentucky Governor Matt Bevin stated, "America does not have a gun problem it has a society problem." He called gun violence a "cultural problem," and he urged Americans, "to wake up and recognize that school shootings are a consequence of a degrading public morality."

He continued, "You cannot legislate evil. We have become desensitized to death; we have become desensitized to killing; we have become desensitized to empathy for our fellow man; it's coming at an extraordinary price, and we have got to look at the root cause of this."

"We can't celebrate death in video games," Bevin continued, "celebrate death in TV shows, celebrate death in movies, celebrate death in musical lyrics, and not remove any sense of morality."

I have to add to his comments, *"celebrate death in War."* America has a "War-fatigued" population that, for almost two generations, has been constantly at war, according to Wikipedia. **The US has been involved in over 60 military actions since 1990.** They have had prolonged engagements in both Iraq and Afghanistan, with death and destruction the lead on their nightly newscasts. They have had to suffer the negative social-economic impact and the stress of separated and uprooted families and returning veterans, either in body bags or failing to assimilate back in to society.

I am also going to add, *"celebrate the militarization of their police forces."* In an effort to utilize the tremendous military surplus from Iraq, the federal government has downloaded the equipment to local police departments. Every backwater police department is now fully equipped with assault weapons, full military wardrobes, helmets, body armour, night vision equipment, armoured personnel vehicles, and all the latest military surplus. The police forces have become paramilitary storm troopers.

CHAPTER 17

Why is my Grandpa now wrong?

For the past few weeks, "The Wolf Debate" has filled the local papers. Everyone has an opinion. Here's mine!

The Ministry of Natural Resources and Forestry has banned the hunting and trapping of wolves in an effort to protect the Algonquin Wolf, and are working on a recovery strategy.

The Village of Sundridge Council passed a motion asking to extend the comment period of the recovery strategy, but it was rejected by the MNRF.

Ray Gall, VP of the Ontario Fur Managers Federation, has done a series of Letters to the Editors. "APEX PREDATOR PROTECTION IRRESPONSIBLE" was a well-reasoned, rational and factual article questioning the science behind the MNRF efforts, and even the genetic existence of the Algonquin Wolf.

Wolves are large carnivores—the largest member of the dog, or canid, family. Domestic dogs evolved from the wolf.

I have tremendous respect for wolves.

I am neither a wolf hater nor a wolf lover. They are the top predator and have to be good at their job to survive. But I do believe the local population is mutating.

Humans are predisposed to fear and hate wolves; every nursery rhyme uses them as a threat for children's misbehaviour. There is no one my age that can't sing the tune:

Who's afraid of the big bad wolf
Big bad wolf, big bad wolf?
Tra la la la la.

My lifelong view on wolves was solidified as a teenager by a school project.

It was the mid-sixties; the deer herd and the beaver population had been decimated by a number of severe winters. Then as now, the discussions raged on whether the wolves were to blame. There were no coyotes in the area.

I decided Timber Wolves would be the topic of my school project… five minutes in front of the class talking about wolves, with visual displays.

Five o'clock on a February morning, and I had procrastinated as usual. I was sitting at the kitchen table finishing it up; my school project was due that day.

Grandpa came down to start the wood cook stove (the only source of heat in that end of the house). He worked his magic opening the dampers, stuffing his secret mixture of newspaper and kindling into the firebox, struck the wood match on the seat of his mackinaw pants; the fire was ablaze, the coffee was on. If I had done it, the house would have been full of smoke.

"Grandpa, you have spent your life working in the bush, hunting and guiding—what can you tell me about wolves?"

"Well son," he said as he lit his pipe, and settled down on a wooden chair. "I can tell Yeh, you will never see one in the bush! I have seen ones that have been trapped, but I've never seen a live one."

No sir… you will never see one. You will hear them howl at night; you'll hear them yipping or you'll hear the leaves crunching as they follow or circle you in the bush; you will be able to sense them when they are near, and the hair on the back of your neck will stand up. On a damp day, you will be able to smell them. You will see their tracks or a kill site… but no sir, you will never see one." He puffed on his pipe and finished up. "They are cautious, sly and shy around humans, they will see you, but you will never see them."

He was right for over fifty years, but not now.

There was no Google in those days. All my research was done the old-fashioned way. My grandmother was an old school "marm," and actually had two different full sets of thirty-some volumes each of encyclopedias, and a set of wildlife books.

Some of you will remember "Hinterlands Who's Who" from the sixties, public service messages profiling Canadian animals. After one of their episodes on the Wolf, I wrote a letter and requested a package. I also wrote a request to the Department of Lands and Forest. Within a couple of weeks, I got big brown envelopes back, chock full of pictures and info.

My research indicated that there were three different types of wolf in our area: the grey or timber wolf, the red wolf, and the eastern wolf. The adults are about 5-6 feet long and weighed up to 175 lb. They all had the same colour range, from all white to all black, and every combination thereof. They are very social, living in family packs with an alpha male and alpha female; she is the only one to bear pups, but they are nurtured by all. If food was scarce, there were no litters.

They are the apex predator, opportunistic hunters and cannibalistic. (The injured or weak in the pack become lunch.) They can eat about twenty lbs of meat at a sitting. The Alphas eat first. Meals are few and far between. Their primary diet is rodents, small animals, beaver, deer, and sometime moose. The mortality and injury rate of the wolves during a moose hunt is extremely high. They are nocturnal, and usually hunt at night.

Over the last few years, I have seen a number of wolves in the wild. This past deer season, on two different days and at different locations, our hunters had encounters with wolves. One hunter was sitting on the ground, leaning against a tree and two came up to within ten feet and only bolted when they were yelled at. The other hunter had two come right up; they passed him on his watch. They were on a set of tracks. Four others were off in the distance.

Why is my Grandpa now wrong? Why are we seeing them now? Why are we seeing them during the day? Why have they lost that caution and shyness? Why are we seeing so many?

I believe Wolves are now evolving in reverse. They are interbreeding with coyotes and domestic dogs. They are losing their ability to regulate their own populations, and have lost the fear or caution of people.

That's my view from the porch.

CHAPTER 18

The wildlife trade of the century

We are going to talk turkey!

Not your Thanksgiving or Christmas "butterball" variety, but

The Eastern Wild Turkey (Meleagis gallopava silvestris)

Wild Turkeys disappeared from Ontario's fields and forest in 1909, but I saw some yesterday!

I was cruising across HWY 124, and I came upon a pickup stopped in front of me in the middle of the road. Thinking someone was in distress, I cautiously pulled up beside him. I rolled down the passenger side window, and asked. *"Do you need some help?"*

With a big smile on his face and pointing over his hood, he replied, *"NO! But thanks for stopping; I have been watching them! They strutted right across the road; I had to stop for them."* Off on the edge of the ditch were six turkeys, two of the males, fans out full, in the middle of a mating dance.

The turkey's reintroduction back in 1980s has been a success; it's surpassed anyone's expectations. They have expanded way beyond their original range and are now as far north as Nipissing.

Trading fifty Algonquin moose for turkeys has unquestionably created a boon to hunting activities and wildlife observation opportunities. The National Wild Turkey Federation (now the

Canadian Wild Turkey Federation—https://cwtf.ca/), the MNRF and Ontario Federation of Anglers & Hunters, (OFAH) all played major roles in the reintroduction.

One expert's comment summed it up, "It just might have been the wildlife trade of the century."

A total of 274 turkeys were released at locations throughout southeastern Ontario. As those turkeys flourished, the MNR began trapping the turkeys and moving them further away from their original drop points, establishing new populations. The rest is history. The population is increasing exponentially. It is estimated that within the next year, the turkey population, excluding the Queen's Park and Ottawa subspecies, will exceed 120,000.

There are now some concerns that they will over-populate and have a negative effect on the ecosystem. They are seed and nut eaters, and there is some concern that they may be eating other ground nesting birds' eggs, such as partridge eggs. If you talk to a farmer in southwest Ontario, he will be crying about how much crop damage they do.

We have just passed the thirtieth anniversary of Ontario's legal hunts for wild turkey; the hunt started in the spring of 1987 in WMU 68 & 71 in Renfrew County. And there is now even a local season. There are now spring and fall seasons.

There were just over 7,000 birds harvested in 2017 in Ontario. One management report I read indicated that the birds can sustain a 10% harvest rate, any less than that may lead to over-population.

There are five different subspecies of turkeys in North America; the eastern is now the most predominate. If you are a turkey hunter, your ultimate dream, challenge, or goal is to get the *"Grand Slam"*—harvest one of each species.

The toms are substantially larger than the females, with large, featherless, reddish head, red throat, and red wattles on the throat and neck. Males typically have a "beard," a tuft of coarse hair (modified feathers) growing from the center of the breast. The beards average 230 mm (9.1 in) in length. Tom weighs from 5 to 11 kg (11 to 24 lb) and measures 100-125 cm (39-49 in) in length

THAT DOG DON'T HUNT

The record wild turkey harvested weighed 16.85 kg (37.1 lb).

Juvenile males are called Jakes; a juvenile is distinguished by a very short beard, and its tail fan has longer feathers in the middle. The adult male's tail fan feathers will be all the same length.

Males may be seen courting in groups, often with the dominant male gobbling, spreading its tail feathers (strutting), drumming/booming, and spitting. Males will mate with as many hens as they can to ensure their genes are carried on.

Male turkeys are polygamous and exhibit strong sexual dimorphism. That is; *they like to strut their stuff*. When males are excited, in addition to fanning those stunning red, purple, green, copper, bronze, and gold tail feathers, they puff out their feathers and drag their wings, the fleshy flap on the bill expands, and the wattles and the bare skin of the head and neck all become engorged with blood, almost concealing the eyes and bill.

Courtship begins during the months of March and April, which is when turkeys are still flocked together in winter areas.

Hens nest in shallow dirt depressions hidden in woody vegetation. Hens lay a clutch of 10-14 eggs, usually one per day. The eggs are incubated for at least 28 days. The poults leave the nest in about 12-24 hours.

The hen's feathers are duller overall, in shades of brown and gray. The primary wing feathers have white bars. The hen is typically much smaller than the tom, at 2.5-5.4 kg (5.5-11.9 lb).

I haven't counted them, but turkeys have 5000 to 6000 feathers. Each foot has three toes in front, with a shorter, rear-facing toe in back; males have a spur at the back of each of their lower legs.

Most people are familiar with the term "flock of pigeons" and even "gaggle of geese," but did you know that a group of turkeys is called a **"rafter"**? And baby turkeys are called **poults**.

Turkeys have extremely sharp eyesight and are natural sprinters. They can outrun any of their predators. However, despite their weight, and unlike their domestic cousins, they are agile fliers. They fly back and forth from their perches or roosts and will fly close to the ground for up to 400 metres (a quarter mile).

Since we are talking turkey hunting, in next month's column, I will have to tell you about **the most expensive hunt I have never been on.**

CHAPTER 19

The most expensive hunt I have never been on.

Last time we talked turkey.

Now let's talk about the most expensive hunt I have never been on.

As an impressionable youth, I envied our fellow hunters south of the border. They had turkeys to hunt. I was obsessed. Every time I passed a magazine rack, every hunting magazine (all of them American), had an article on turkey hunting, and I studied every one of them. I was schooled; I could have given lessons on how to hunt turkey. For years I had crates and boxes full of magazines. $$$

I was going to be a Turkey Hunter!

It was a priority!

It was going to happen!

I was going to save my pennies and head to the states for a hunt. In fact, on a newlywed winter excursion to Florida in the mid-1970s I made some contacts to set up a hunt for later in the spring. It didn't happen! Changing diapers became the priority.

For the second time, in the early 80s, and with all the ads in the hoard of magazines that I had gathered, I began a two-year process of planning a hunt in Pennsylvania, (too many crawly creatures in Florida for my liking, LOL). There were endless hours of expensive telephone calls, postage for letters, and toward the end of the process, fax communications. **$$$** And again, life got in the way.

When we traded those moose for turkeys, I was ecstatic with the news we were going to be able hunt turkeys at home here in Ontario. For the third time, I prepared for a hunt.

I was going to be ready for the spring hunt of 1988. In prep for the hunt, I trekked down to Renfrew County twice to do a pre-hunt scout, **$$$,** bought two books and a video on Turkey hunting, **$$$,** bought a complete set of turkey camo, boots, pants, shirts, hat, and mask, along with some face blackening—just in case. I bought two different types of calls, and spent hours practicing. **$$$. Oh Yeah! Did I mention the new shotgun? $$$**

Until just recently, to get a Turkey license you had to take a prescribed course and pass an exam.

If memory serves, at that time the only course available was at the **OFAH** (Ontario Federation of Anglers and Hunters) in Peterborough. I signed up, paid my money to take the course, and reserved a motel room; all non-refundable, **$$$**. A family crisis intervened and I couldn't attend.

I tried two other times to take the course and exam, **$$$**. The last time, I just had to order the disc and study it, and then make an appointment to write the exam. I never did.

I have procrastinated long enough… now I can just walk in and buy my license.

Fast forward to 2018. True to my procrastinating nature, 42 years after my first attempt, we are in the middle of the spring turkey hunt, and I still haven't hunted turkeys. But I have been adding up the cost. **$$$**

Thirty years of membership dues to the NWTF (National Wild Turkey and the Canadian Wild Turkey Federation), **$$$**; attendance at NWTF fundraisers and conventions, **$$$**; I was active in the steering committee for the formation of the Canadian Turkey Federation, **$$$**.

There is a reason they sell alcohol before the bidding at the fundraisers. You bid on things you would never normally want. The song lyrics, *"closing time at the bar… all the girls are a ten,"* certainly applies to your judgement when bidding at fundraising auctions.

If you look around my home, the walls are covered with huge NWTF prints; there is a large ugly turkey adorned flower vase in the corner. We have turkey logoed carryalls, platters, and mugs. I have three consecutively larger sizes of NWTF denim shirts and Melton cloth and leather jackets, an array of NWTF hats, and much more, $$$. I can't even recoup the costs at a garage sale—seems no one wants them.

Accepting how keen a turkey's eyesight is and recognizing my inability to sit still for any length of time, I purchased a camo surround blind so they couldn't bust me, $$$. (I set it up a couple of times deer hunting.) It eventually just rotted away. I then purchased a pop-up blind so I was completely hidden (never used… it's for sale if anyone is looking for one), $$$.

Strolling through one of the big box sporting goods stores, one of my buddies twisted my arm… if I was going to hunt turkey, I needed to buy a big propane turkey deep fryer to enjoy the harvest, $$$. I think I cooked one Thanksgiving butterball in it. After 25 years of neglect, I finally had to throw it out last year.

I bought a new camo 2¾-inch 12-gauge shotgun back in 1988 for that first hunt, $$$. Over the years the marketing gurus convinced us that if we were going to hunt turkeys, we should change to 3-inch and bigger shells, and to shotguns specifically designed for turkey hunting. Over the years I upgraded turkey guns twice more, $$$.

As any novice turkey hunter will tell you, when hunting turkey, you have to be still and well hidden. I have taken that as gospel. However, to accommodate constantly changing spring weather, and to maximize your hunting comfort, it is essential that you have both light and heavyweight camo gear. In addition to the original purchase of the camo hunting gear, as I have matured (that is a euphemism for gained weight), I now have three complete sets of camo, in medium, large and extra-large, $$$.

I was recently talking to a fellow hunter who had just returned from an African safari. He had really enjoyed the experience and hunt, but was whining about the cost. Not to be out done, I reminded him what I had spent **$$$** over the years on **a turkey hunt that I have never been on.**

At least he got to Africa.

My wife says I can't spend any more money, but maybe I'll get turkey hunting next year.

CHAPTER 20

"That dog don't hunt!"

"That dog don't hunt!"

Well! I hadn't heard that phrase in ages.

It's an expression my grandfather used.

A quick Google search traced its origin to Texas, and said it was popularized in a 1991 movie, *JFK*.

I am calling BS on that. I can remember it from my childhood.

The Hunt Camp Porch "dictionary" defines it as an old English expression that migrated with the early settlers.

It is a sarcastic expression used to refer to something that is not likely to happen, or to something that is as useless as a hound that won't hunt. For example, my grandfather would tell me to do my chores, and my great uncle would chortle, *"That dog don't hunt!"*

Let me tell you about a dog that wouldn't hunt.

I love deer hunting with hounds. Their barking and baying, off in the distance, then coming closer and closer, creates a sense of anticipation and an adrenalin rush like nothing else.

Truth be known, I have hunted more years without hounds than with them. Despite my best efforts, *"That dog don't hunt,"* has become a statement of fact.

In the seventies, as our gang solidified, the decision was made to get some hunting dogs. No expense was to be spared. We were going to have the best hunters anyone had ever seen.

In the interim, we decided to rent a hound. We tasked one of the guys with finding one. He scoured the local watering holes till he found an old codger that just happened to have a hunting dog, at an enormous fee, and according to him:

"I'll be happy to take your money. King is in great shape… pure blue tick… you won't find a better dog. I fed King all year and I won't be able to hunt this year… hard working dog, doesn't run anything but deer… shot three deer in front of him last year."

We built an oversized, insulated dog house, picked up a bale of straw bedding, a 50 lb bag of dog food, and a big box of bacon flavoured treats. This dog, in keeping with its name was going to be treated royally. For years that doghouse was referred to as "Kings Castle."

Sunday afternoon on the way into the camp we stopped to pick up King.

King was not as advertised. He was a mangy, flea bitten, foul smelling mongrel of undefined lineage. No royalty there.

We tried to put him in the box of the truck—"*That dog don't hunt!*" He wanted to ride in the cab. Just about to the camp, King passed gas… the foulest, most eye-watering, gagging odour ever. Opening the windows wasn't enough… we had to stop and open the doors. That was King's chance to escape. He sauntered down the road, leading the way to camp.

Within sight of camp, two rabbits crossed the road in front of him; he was off. For three hours, he was back and forth, doing ever widening circles around the camp, barking and chasing something. The rabbits showed back up at camp about ½ hour after King took off. King continued his search. No amount of calling would get him to stop.

Finally, at dusk he wandered back into camp, soaking wet, covered in mud, tongue hanging out, exhausted and somewhat worse for wear with paws bleeding.

We got King fed and bedded down in his Castle. Near midnight, just as we all settled into our beds, from the castle came the most sorrowful homesick whiney howl you can imagine. It kept up all night. None of us got any sleep.

Opening morning, one look at King, you knew he wasn't going anyplace, worn out from his rabbit experience. We left him to rest.

The second night the sorrowful howling continued. It was fraying everyone's nerves. Finally, about three am, someone got up and brought King into the camp. He snuggled in close to the wood stove and all was quiet.

Tuesday morning, I gave one of the hunters a handful of the bacon treats to use to lure the dog in case he got by the line of hunters.

I took King to the bush. He seemed eager. But no! I started the run. He was continually underfoot... would not go more than ten feet away, not a bark out of him. Near the end of the run King stopped in his tracks, raised his nose, sniffed the air, yelped and took off.

Finally! We could see what he could do. He disappeared with that one yelp. Not another sound.

I got out to the hunter with the treats, and there was King, curled up at his feet chewing on a bacon treat.

The second run was even further away from the truck. The rest of the gang repositioned themselves on stands about a half mile away. They signalled us they were in place. We took off to give King another chance to prove himself.

He ran back and forth between me and the treat guy... then he was gone. I assumed he had just stayed with the treats. I got out to the line, gathered up the hunters and headed to meet the treat guy. No King. He thought the dog was with me.

A lost dog causes a gamut of emotions: worry about their safety, frustration at the interrupted hunt, and anger for letting it happen.

After a quick lunch, still no sign of King. We were about two miles from the truck. We decided the hunters would sit in one spot and head back to the camp about four pm. The treat guy and I would search for King back toward the truck. And maybe scare something out to the gang.

Yelling and whistling for the dog, we worked our way back toward the truck, zig-zagging back and forth, all the time, getting more concerned. No King!

Exhausted and now near dark we arrived back at the truck. There was King fast asleep under the truck. Not too gently, I threw him into the truck and immediately drove him home.

I only thing I said to the owner:

"That dog don't hunt!"

CHAPTER 21

That Dog Still Won't Hunt

On occasion I will get an email, call, or text from readers sharing their stories or commenting on how they enjoyed or didn't like one of the articles. Last month topped the charts. I now have enough material and dog stories to last for about three years of columns.

I can remember, as a youngster, a large painting or print of mounted riders. One had a bugle to his mouth ready to signal the start… and a huge pack of hounds excitedly milling about the horses waiting for the hunt to begin. I remember gazing at it over and over again with envy. I wanted to hunt with dogs! I still love to hunt with dogs.

My first experience deer hunting with dogs, in the early 1970s, coincided with my first stay at a real hunt camp. I got an invitation to hunt at the "Old Balsam School House" with the Irwin Gang. I was pumped!

That experience and the stories from that camp will stay with me forever. I will share some of those stories in the future. We will start with this story.

My Great Uncle, the oldest of the bunch, was the hunt master and the dogger. He carried a bugle to announce the start of the hunt and release of the dog. (This was just like the picture). The dog, as I remember was of mixed pedigree, and at first glance was the least likely hunter you could imagine, but proof of that old adage, **"You can't judge a book by its cover."**

Opening morning I was placed on the highest outcropping of solid Canadian granite in the township. It was well below freezing. I was underdressed. There was no cover; there wasn't even any moss on the rocks. It had to be the coldest, north westerly, laziest November wind on record. I stood there shivering, and wishing I was someplace else.

(A lazy wind as defined in the hunt camp dictionary and according to my Father-in-law is "a wind that is so lazy it doesn't go around you, but straight through you.")

The bugle blared and the dog started to howl, coming closer, then farther away, then back toward me. Right toward me! Wow! What an adrenalin rush. I wasn't shivering from cold anymore, but from excitement.

I could hear a deer crashing through the brush down off the side of the rock to my right, but I couldn't get a look at it. The dog was way behind. Disappointed is not a strong enough word. I missed my chance! I was concentrating on listening for the deer that had gone by when there was a flash of brown off to left. I turned quickly, there was another deer. Bang! I had harvested my first deer in front of a dog. I was hooked.

Now fast forward fifteen years. For all that time I had been asking, *"Honey can we get a hound? Please! Please!"*

Then one spring morning… it was a yes. Before she changed her mind, I headed for the Humane Society pound, driving through a terrible thunderstorm all the way to see what was available.

That was the beginning of multiple, ill-fated attempts to breed and raise Beagles.

You may see a trend here—over the years we have had Thunder 1, Thunder 2, Lighting 1 & 2, Storm and Cloud. "That Dog won't Hunt" applied to all of them.

I got to the pound, and as luck would have it, there was an incredible looking two-year-old female Beagle. *"I'll take it; I am going to name her Thunder."* I blurted out without hesitation as the thunder rumbled outside.

Perfect! It was finally going to happen. I had my dog. Breeding 101: if you are going to breed dogs, start with a female. I was happy. I was going to have a pack of dogs within a couple of years. The best deer hounds in the district.

On the way home, Thunder howled insistently, tore up the back seat with her claws and chewed the arm rest. It was an omen of things to come.

I built her a state-of-the-art insulated dog house and a steel-fenced run in the back yard. I took her to the vet, got her all checked out, rabies shot, assorted other shots, and de-worming medicine. I think I paid the vet's mortgage for the month. No expense was spared.

Thunder wouldn't go near the dog house. If you left her in the run she howled and howled, to the point where all the neighbours complained. Apparently, she was a house dog, but not necessarily house-trained. The only time she would get off the couch was to eat or escape out the door. She terrorized the neighbourhood. She never ran deer, but would chase every kid on a bike, and every car that went by. She chewed the legs off of just about every piece of furniture in the house. My wife was not pleased.

Undeterred, I waited and waited for her to come into heat to get her bred. I failed breeding 101. A word of caution, if you are going get a dog for breeding, make sure it hasn't been spayed—so much for raising beagles.

Finally hunting season arrived, and out to the bush we went. For a week, she would never stray more than ten feet away from me. To her credit, she did bark and howl as we walked through the bush. At one point I jumped a deer out of its bed about 100 feet in front of me. Thunder yelped and ran around behind me, hiding. It became pretty clear… "That Dog won't Hunt."

After hunting season, I found her a nice home with an elderly couple out on a farm.

That was my first failed attempt at raising beagles. It took a few more years to talk my wife into trying it again. That's a story for another column.

CHAPTER 22

Memories

My wife maintains there are only two seasons at our house. "*Hunting season and getting ready for hunting season.*" Not so much this year. It's mid-September and I haven't started to get ready. Normally, I am bear hunting by now.

Back in May, we bought a seasonal trailer in a park on Ahmic Lake. We spent an incredible summer here. The boys bought me a pair of bottle-bottom-thick glasses, and they now call me "Bubbles." (This is a "Trailer Park Boys" reference.)

I want to share a few memories and stories with you. These stories are recalled with fondness, respect, and admiration.

I first met Gerry in the fall of 1977. I can't remember if it was deer or moose season. He and a group had bought the 800 acres of land abutting the 700 acres at the hunt camp. We invited him to hunt with us.

I picked him up with my 4 X 4 at his house on a Sunday morning to take him to the hunt camp. It was the beginning of forty years of friendship. In all those years, I never heard him use a cuss word. His expletive was, *"Ah Mitch."*

Gerry used a Winchester Model 70 in 30-06 with an Aimpoint scope. The morning I picked him up, he had just bought a new box of shells. When health and age forced him to quit hunting a few years back, he still had 14 shells. But he had shot six moose. He never carried a loaded gun. He would just put one shell in if needed.

Gerry was directionally challenged. He endured a lot of good-natured teasing. He was apprehensive about being in the bush, but he always wanted to go. In the early years, he carried a survival kit with food for a day, a space blanket, water proof matches, and a fold-up 22 survival gun. He never had to use it, but it was close a couple of times.

He always carried two compasses, one in his pocket, and the other clipped to the metal zipper of his jacket. He could never understand why north was always pointing to his chest.

He was well-known as the moose magnet. One year, deer hunting, we had finished a run, and George and I headed down the trail to meet Gerry. We turned a corner and there he was walking up the trail, his head down, stepping around a flood on the trail—unaware two moose were following him, about 100 feet behind.

His favourite lunch was a foul-smelling blue cheese and German summer sausage, with a thick slice of onion, on heavy German rye bread. (Early on, we never let him bring the cheese into the camp—it smelled so bad).

We were a bunch of good old country boys whose idea of diversifying was to buy Schneider's bologna instead of Maple Leaf. Most of us had never eaten anything but white bread. Gerry introduced us to a whole new world. A 25 lb loaf of Dimpflmeier's dark rye, sliced onions, and a variety of summer sausages are now a staple on the camp lunch table. You may even find blue cheese in the fridge.

Toward the end of the week, he would cook up a cabbage goulash, using up all the leftovers. The first time he cooked it, we hesitated about eating it. It wasn't meat and potatoes. In later years, we looked forward to it.

We had left him on the road with the truck; he was sitting on the tailgate eating his lunch. George and I were going to circle around, make a short run and come back to him. We weren't gone but minutes when we heard a shot from the direction of the truck, and moose crashing through the bush not far from us.

THAT DOG DON'T HUNT

We got back to Gerry and there was a moose lying on the road at the back of the truck. He excitedly told us the story. "Ah Mitch… you wouldn't believe it. You just left and I went around the front of the truck to relieve myself, I looked up and there were three moose at the tail gate. One was sniffing my sandwich. I had to shoo them away. I loaded my gun and shot the closest one."

Back in my bear articles, I talked about one of the gang that stepped on a hibernating bear. It was Gerry. He came out of the bush, his face white from fright; he was covered in snow, and his hat was gone. He blurted, *"Ah Mitch… I stepped on a bear. It was under the snow. It jumped up and knocked me over."*

Every morning at the camp he would go down to the lake and swim, some years breaking ice. We shivered just watching him.

If you look up **enduring adversity** in the dictionary Gerry's name would pop up.

Gerry and his wife Ilse emigrated from Germany in the 1960s. They struggled to learn a new language and customs. As a child, Gerry survived the food shortages and the 1930s depression in Germany, often going hungry. Late in the war, at the age of fifteen, he was shanghaied into the German Navy to man a shore battery. The stories he told. Being a skinny young kid, the used uniforms he was issued were four sizes too big, his boots two sizes too big. *"Ah Mitch, I had blisters on my feet the whole time. My great coat had bullet holes in it. I was scared the whole time."*

He survived a couple of bouts of cancer, and wore a Urostomy bag. He lost a cherished fifteen-year-old son to a lightning strike. In later years, Alzheimer's began to take its toll. His cheerfulness and zest for life never wavered. He inspired us all. Last week I attended Gerry's celebration of life and said goodbye to a friend, neighbour, and hunting buddy.

Gerhard Emil Schulte, September 29, 1928- August 30, 2018

Over the last short while I have said goodbye to two others of the original hunters.

I think that has had more of impact on my desire to go hunting than the good life at the trailer park.

CHAPTER 23

Camo. It snuck up on me; I didn't see it coming.

Camo has gone main stream. It's not just in the hunter's closet anymore.

Over the last couple of weeks, I have seen it.

My new daughter-in-law hosted a camo-themed Thanksgiving. A trip to the variety store revealed three young high school girls in full designer camo; jackets, tights, backpacks, boots, and even headbands.

On a recent trip down to the post office, I walked by the display window of our local seamstress. There, for all to see, was a winter white camo wedding dress, and alongside it were camo evening dresses: one in a Realtree forest green pattern, and the other a pink camo.

Heading out the door to the hardware store, I got that look from my wife, and the question all men get. *"You are not going to wear that, are you?"* I had committed a fashion faux pas—my camo jacket and pants clashed.

Now it seems it wasn't that long ago you wouldn't have found a Canadian hunter even wearing camo. Our hunting culture transitioned from red plaid to the hunter orange (formerly called blaze orange) when it became law, effective September 1, 1997.

THAT DOG DON'T HUNT

The two largest American camo companies, Realtree and Mossey Oaks, both evolved in 1986 to meet the needs of the American bow hunters. The early camo was designed for the warm southern US climate, and not Canada's colder climate. Realtree has a unique business plan; they don't manufacture any products, just license the patented designs to other manufacturers.

My first up-close encounter with camo was in the late 80s. A group from the hunt camp would go on an annual fly-in or lodge fishing excursion. We had picked a water access American plan resort (meals are supplied) on Dollars Lake out by the S narrows on Hwy 522. We were unloading the boats at the resort dock, when in behind us came a 16 ft square-fronted Jon boat. The boat, motor, all the gear, and the individuals were camo'd. We were standing there in blue jeans and t-shirts.

We ended up sharing a dinner table with them for the duration of the trip. They were two good ole boys from Arkansas; Bubba and his cousin Bubba—(Yea, that's right). They were the stereotypical southern redneck. We were amused by their slow southern drawl and teased them about their wardrobe. We were probably a little envious. Head to toe everything was camo. They boasted that even their underwear was camo. They claimed that the eyesight of the walleye was so keen the camo would help them catch fish.

They were there to catch Walleye and used night crawlers for bait; we were there to catch Pickerel and used dew worms. Who was counting, but we got far more fish than they did!

Nature's camo is amazing. A young fawn born with white spots is almost invisible when it's lying down. The black hide and white legs of a 1500 lb moose, like magic, can make it disappear in a few steps in a boreal forest.

I got squirreled, my ADD was in full bloom researching the evolution of the use of camouflage; it was an eye-opener. I must have read a thousand pages to compose this thousand-word column.

The use and development of military camouflage has had a mottled history. It was first used by the world's navies until the advent of radar, which made the use of marine camo redundant.

Over the years "dazzle patterns" (blotches or stripes of paint) were used. There was no science behind it.

The Romans camouflaged their ships when they attacked England in 55 BC. They painted them the same colour as the sea.

British destroyers in the Mediterranean were painted "Mountbatten Pink" in 1940. Louis Mountbatten noticed a civilian cruise ship in pink tones disappear on the horizon. He had his fleet painted a mixture of red and grey, thinking it would reduce their silhouettes during dawn and dusk.

Until the last few decades, camo for ground troops was not needed. Historically, it was just the opposite. On the Plains of Abraham, the British wore scarlet red, and the French wore royal blue. It made it easy to see who you were shooting at.

In 1939, Germany researched and developed a forest pattern camo for their SS troops; it was ahead of its time and was the most effective camo invented until the development of the new Canadian Disruptive Pattern, CADPAT. It's now the benchmark for all military camo—the best in the world!

I talked with retired Maj. Doug Palmer who headed the Canadian Forces "Clothe the Soldier" project in the 90s.

He stated, "The Canadian Army was the first to take an analytic and science-based approach to the development of temperate woodlands camo, based on both visible and infrared spectrums. They came up with an algorithm-based computer-generated four-colour-pattern that optimized concealment from the naked eye, enhanced optics up to three power, and active night vision devices for significantly reduced detection in the 50-300 metre range.

We even factored in the different soldiers' physical sizes and body shapes, and the effect on the pattern. There was a tremendous amount of research in developing the combination of cloth materials and colour adhesion."

The new combat uniforms were adopted by the Canadian Forces in 1997 and remain the best and most effective camo in use.

The US Marine Corp expressed interest, and Canada shared the pattern with them.

THAT DOG DON'T HUNT

I read a blog that stated with some authority that the US army, to avoid the patent, put their logo on, made some changes to the camo colouring, and adopted it for their use. The changes, however, greatly reduced the effectiveness of the pattern.

Just for the record, despite my wife's protest, I did go to the hardware with the clashing camo. She was disgusted. LOL

CHAPTER 24

It's a Gang problem, Not a Gun Problem

It's early on a Monday morning as I sit on the camp porch in front of my computer to share with you a story about the humorous happenings at the hunt camp. I GOT SQUIRRELED... For the first time all summer, the TV is on, and for some reason it's tuned to CP 24, the Toronto news channel. To my astonishment, there had been three shootings in Toronto over the weekend (all gang related). I am appalled, and at the same time, frustrated. I am going to rant and share my thoughts on the Liberal's misdirected efforts on gun control, and the impact it will have on you and me, and our firearms heritage.

I'm frustrated that you and I... the responsible trustworthy gun owners, hunters, trappers, sports shooters, and collectors—2.2 million of us (that's more Canadian men and women than play Hockey)—are held responsible for these shootings, and are going to suffer the consequences. Not the criminals.

Back in June, before Parliament recessed for the summer, **Trudeau's Liberals passed Bill C-71**. If you are like 95% of the hunters/gun owners in Canada, you are going to ask **"What's that?"**

It's a new firearms law that has passed, but doesn't come into effect till after the upcoming federal election. Among a number of other onerous regulations, it gives the government the arbitrary, unhindered ability to confiscate your guns. No valid reason, no oversight.

Bill Blair, former Toronto Police Chief and now Liberal MP for Scarborough and Minister of Border Security and Organized Crime pledged the biggest single gun seizures in Canadian history. He indicated that if re-elected, **the Liberals will start with the confiscation of 200,000 unrestricted rifles and shotguns** (that could be your hunting rifles), and then move on to confiscating handguns.

I am going to be as blunt as I can:

"If you are a firearms owner and vote Liberal on October 21… you deserve to lose your guns."

My motivation for making this statement is completely selfish… I want my boys, and my granddaughter and grandson to be able to continue to own and use guns responsibly and enjoy our hunting heritage.

Canada does not have a gun problem… It has a drug and gang problem!

All three of the Toronto shootings this past weekend were gang related. **Bill C-71**, the new gun law does nothing to address gang violence.

A while back, a gentleman named Nicolas Johnson started **TheGunBlog.ca**. He is a voice of reason in the wilderness, and his blog is the most comprehensive source of what is happening politically to our firearms. Check it out! Below are some edited excerpts from his August 2019 blog.

Trudeau […] and allies are ramping up efforts to criminalize the country's safest and most-lawful citizens and take away their firearms.

The Canadian Association of Chiefs of Police, which lobbies the government to restrict hunters and sport shooters, doesn't support new gun bans against them, The Canadian Press reported today, citing the CACP president.

Toronto Police Chief Mark Saunders and at least five other active and retired Canadian police leaders have a message for politicians campaigning to ban guns from hunters, farmers and sport shooters:

"**No.**" said Saunders yesterday, declining to support Prime Minister Justin Trudeau's marketing for massive bans to win votes.

Adam Palmer, also the Vancouver police chief, is among at least six active and retired police leaders who oppose the mass confiscations sought by Justin Trudeau.

Palmer said Canada's laws are already strong and no other law is needed, The Canadian Press said in an article published on the website of CTV News.

The country has strict punishments for people who use firearms and ammunition for violence. "In every single case there are already offences for that," Palmer was quoted as telling The Canadian Press. "They're already breaking the law, and the criminal law in Canada addresses all of those circumstances."

"The firearms laws in Canada are actually very good right now, Palmer was quoted as saying today at the end of the CACP's annual conference in Calgary. "They're very strict."

Attacking trustworthy gun owners does not solve the gang problem. The conservative election platform outlines a comprehensive plan to effectively attack the gang violence… check it out.

"Common Sense on Firearms" from Conservative leader Andrew Scheer (Source: www.AndrewScheer.com)

"In my mind, a successful firearms policy should do two things. It should deter criminal activity and should respect the rights of law-abiding gun owners. For too long, laws in this country have had it backwards. Bills crafted in downtown offices by people who often had no first-hand experience using firearms have put undue restrictions on those who respect and follow the law, while doing virtually nothing to stop the criminals who ignore it."

Canadian voters in general, and gun owners in particular, are world renowned for their political apathy and complacency, and make an easy target for the politicians.

As CEO of the Canadian Firearms Institute, a resource and advocacy group for firearms owners, I experienced that complacency, with frustration, on a regular basis.

Hunters use their guns for a couple of weeks a year, put them away, and don't give them much thought till the next season. Give them some thought… next season you may not have them.

There are 2.2 million legal men and women gun owners in Canada. They are not all of one political persuasion. They echo the general voting population, and seldom vote for their guns. If they voted with their guns in mind, they would be an influential political force.

During my political advocacy days, I remember attending a seminar; the theme was how to overcome the Canadian voter's political disengagement and apathy. As a case in point, the facilitator used the example below.

"How do you get 100 Canadians out of a pool on the hottest summer day?" Just yell: "OK, everyone out of the pool."

No one will ask why or refuse… they will get out in an orderly fashion. If you asked anywhere else in the world, there would be a rebellion or disobedience.

On October 21, election day… Tell the Trudeau Liberals, **"I am not getting out of the pool!"**

Update: May 2020: By Order in Council, not an act of Parliament, the Liberal Government arbitrarily banned and prohibited over 1500 varieties of legal rifles, a lot of them hunting guns, and are adding to the list daily. The cost to the taxpayer is estimated in the billions, and the effectiveness is in question. Criminals do not use legal guns. Not only has there been strong opposition to the Order in Council from the gun community, but from unexpected sources, including the Canadian Tax Payers Federation, the Canadian organization of Police Chiefs, the RCMP member union, and a number of other police services.

CHAPTER 25

The Question

What makes you a hunter? Why do you hunt? Why do you enjoy hunting? These are questions that I am constantly asked.

I have never been able to articulate a satisfactory answer. My go-to answer is, "it's in my DNA." At an early age, I didn't realize that hunting was a sport.

My early years of hunting and training were with a generation that hunted to supplement their food supply. They relied on venison to make it through the winter. They had hunted to survive the depression and the meat rations of WWII. It was lean times if they were unsuccessful. Their skill level and preparation for the hunt reflected that reality. Their success or failure defined them.

I posed the above questions to the younger hunters at the supper table this past deer season.

The comments, below, from "Compass" showed up in my in box a couple of weeks later.

"How would you define Hunting? This could be answered in an extensive amount of ways. The perceptions and interpretation, all based on experience and opinions from those whom partake, oppose, or are indifferent.

Some feel this is a barbaric ritual that brings fear, cruelty, and violence. The very thought of it sends them running to "The Facebook" to share their beliefs and influence onto others.

THAT DOG DON'T HUNT

Others feel it is their right to provide for their family and to enjoy the outdoors, as it was meant to be. It's the camaraderie, tradition, and instinct. Man vs. nature, so to speak.

So now I shall share mine.

As a child I was introduced to hunting. Weeks in advance there was the pre-hunt meeting, the sighting of rifles, shopping, making of cowboy cookies, knife sharpening, and a whole lot of anticipation that was contagious.

Old friends, new friends and many stories of the past, as well predictions of the upcoming hunt were shared.

Then my dad would leave!!! Leave me with my mother, who also had great anticipation—to remodel the house, and paint various rooms' different colors, and all out blasphemous behaviour. Yup! I hated hunting! Until…

It happened! I was brought to the camp. I learned from that day forward to present day about nature and about myself. I was hooked.

As a somewhat mature adult now with experience, I would say that you cannot define hunting. It defines you. My good fortune and experiences in the wilderness have defined me. I am a conservationist, I am a protector, I am an ambassador, and I am a provider. Most of all, I belong somewhere.

The world stops and time stands still. The smell fills, not your lungs, but your soul. Your eyes sharpen, and every detail of your surroundings become crisp and clear as it registers the image in your mind. The sounds are deafening even in the silence. This is the moment when the universe comes together.

The rewards are not just the harvest of meat or a trophy; they are purer than a final outcome. They can't be measured, only understood by those who belong, and who have accepted and cherish the ritual.

Sitting around the table for dinner, and taking that moment to look at a table filled by familiar faces together once a year, but who are considered sacred and family. Also noticing those that have gone and who are to be toasted and remembered as hunters.

Some stories have been told every year, and not just for the benefit of the newer hunters, but for the same reason we sing the same Christmas carols at Christmas, or the national anthem before a sporting event. It is just a part of the experience.

Finding that special spot in the bush for the first time, even though you have been there a thousand times because your approach has changed. Things have changed, as has the world, but now you measure differently. Beaver ponds get bigger or smaller, the forest growth is taller or denser. A late summer storm has turned the open hardwoods into a maze of tangled tree tops not passable by man or beast.

There are surprises at every corner, but still that consistency that makes the universe right again. The day to day grind is not even a memory, there are no barriers or social class, and all are measured only by their role as a hunter.

Stories, not just of the big buck or the quarry in question, develop. It is amazing what a group of people can accomplish on a two-hour run, although it would seem mundane in the average day. A dogger may speak of the water in a pond and how it has changed the landscape, or how amazed he was at the fact that he fell in the same bog as last year.

Watchers will describe how a grouse was beside them the whole run, or the noise they heard behind them that had to be a Sasquatch. Perhaps a nattering squirrel scolded them for intruding on their home ground, or a martin decided they wanted to ride an ATV.

Who knows what will transpire, but it will definitely be reported with excitement and enthusiasm as the gang reconvenes for another run, or a meal.

I recently heard a person describing how the brain interprets fun. There is what was described as cheap fun, going to a movie, playing a video game, shopping etc. This stimulates the mind temporarily, but provides no lasting satisfaction. He then described lasting fun. Experiences like being in the remote wilderness for days, despite lousy weather, surviving yet laughing and accomplishing something. This will be sustained despite the endurance and sacrifice. This will be retained in the long-term memory as fun.

THAT DOG DON'T HUNT

Since the beginning of mankind, we were hunters and gatherers. This has changed and that instinct is not in everybody. Entitlement has replaced accomplishment, and respect for our bounty as sustenance and clothing has been replaced by synthetics and mass production.

To justify our existence to those without this make-up is pointless, but to represent it with pride and respect for ourselves is paramount.

Whatever you hunt, however you hunt, wherever you hunt, you belong! You belong to yourself and to the moments past, present, and future. Cherish it! Embrace it! Be proud of who you are! You have inherited perhaps our most primal trait. There is value in that!"

I received more enlightening comments from the guys and the gals in the gang, and I can't wait to share them in future articles.

CHAPTER 26

The camp that eats together stays together

"That's one of the best meals I have ever had," I exclaimed.

"I can't eat this, it's terrible," I uttered under my breath.

Both these statements have been true at the hunt camp table.

Let's talk about kitchen fare at the hunt camp table. It certainly has been different from camp to camp.

Over the years, I have had the opportunity spend time at dozens of camps. I have more vivid memories of those times at the table than the actual time in the bush. I have a theory; no Einstein is safe. I have seen it proven over and over. To par'a'phrase, **"The gang that eats together stays together."**

As I recounted in other columns, when I was a youngster our home was the hunt camp, and we had paid guests. Vivid memories from that time are centered on the dining room table, listening to the stories of the day and enjoying the camaraderie.

Meals at home through the rest of the year were wholesome and nourishing, served at the kitchen table, but prepared according to the rough economic times.

The meals at hunting season were extravagant and surpassed any proud farmer's wife's threshing party, or family Thanksgiving or Christmas feasts.

THAT DOG DON'T HUNT

From childhood to adulthood those were my expectations at a hunt camp.

Any camp is like a family, the importance of sharing that evening meal can't be overstated. It keeps the group together, sharing the events of everyone's lives over the year, the triumphs, the joys, the sorrows, and sharing the events of the day and the good-natured teasing. It all creates the bonding.

I recalled, not too long ago, my first stay a real hunt camp with the "Old Balsam School Gang," and the excitement of harvesting my first deer in front of dogs. My other memories revolve around the table. In keeping with their camp traditions, the venison heart was prepared; it was boiled, then stuffed with the dried homemade bread crusts, seasoned, and then roasted in the wood cook stove oven. It was sliced and used as sandwich meet for the lunches. I have to admit I was a little leery—I had never tried it before—but it was delicious.

They had salvaged all the furnishings for the school house. From a cookery at a logging camp came a huge oversized wood cookstove and a 90-gallon steam boiler that was converted to a wood stove with a flat top grill welded onto it. All were used for cooking, boiling water, and heat. The plank table had to seat about twenty.

One of the hunters had a hog farm and had brought freshly butchered pork chops. They had to be over two inches thick. They were grilled on the flat top, and I can still recall the sizzle of them cooking, and sitting around the plank table. They were the best tasting I have ever had, even to this day.

When we first established our moose camp, we were all of like minds; the food was important. One of the fathers-in-law signed up to be the cook. Garnet was a retired hard rock miner, trapper, and hunter, and lumber camp "Cookie" from Kirkland Lake. The Sunday meal was always a twenty-plus lb turkey with all the trimmings. The leftovers were used as sandwich meat and the carcass was boiled and turned into one of the best homemade soups you will ever find.

He always peeled and cooked ten lb of potatoes for every meal. The leftovers became home fries for breakfast. Every meal featured boiled cabbage and boiled unions. In addition to homemade pies and desserts, there was always the lumber camp staple, a big tin of corn syrup and butter to mix together and sop up with bread.

Monday was usually huge garlic-infused roasted hip of beef or moose, and Tuesday, a gigantic ham. You never left the table hungry and not uttering how good the meal was.

You came through the door at night, the table was set, there were plates of munchies and dinner was served at 6:30 sharp.

Garnet did the cooking, but the gang took turns doing the dishes. By the time the last pot and pan was dried, he would have a low stakes poker game organized. Not only was he a good cook, he was one of the best and luckiest poker players I have ever met. He had a ritual of shoving any folding money winnings into his shirt pocket. It would be bulging by the end of the hunt. We would always offer to pay him for cooking, but he would never accept. He would always chuckle and say, *"You boys can't afford to pay me; I took all your money at poker."*

I visited one camp where everyone individually brought their own grub for the week. There was always someone who didn't bring enough, and had to scrounge off the others. They all ate at different times, and there was a constant squabble—sometimes heated—over who was going to use the barbeque or stove; one would have a gourmet meal, and someone else would have a sandwich. That camp proved my theory. They only lasted about two seasons, and then they all moved on.

Another confirmation of my theory: a new gang I visited only lasted one season. One of the guys known for his spendthrift ways was charged with buying the groceries for the week, but he lacked any prep skills. I think the closest he had ever come to preparing a meal was to question his wife, *"what's for supper."*

He bought all the no-name products, and the cheapest cuts of meats, and he came without a meal plan. The gang had the food, but no one was charged with cooking. There was no refrigeration and everything was left in coolers. I left after two days. I heard that by the Wednesday, they were all deathly ill with food poisoning.

THAT DOG DON'T HUNT

Another camp survived on canned beans or chili and wieners for the week. They changed it up in the morning, and added eggs. They were only together for a short while. By the end of the hunt, the cabin had a distinctive foul odour.

Anyone I have talked to from a long-lasting camp has validated the theory. The quality of food and the shared times around the table has kept them coming back every year.

CHAPTER 27

Different Outcome

In a past article, I shared the story of the moose hunters who hadn't paid attention to the new regulations, and had illegally hunted calves all week out of season; I listed the 2019 dates for the "Tag" draw deadlines for the various hunts—deer, moose, etc.

Make sure you check the new significant changes to the Tag system and hunter reporting. It is now mandatory for hunters to report.

Below is a short version, as outlined in the MNRF quarterly electronic newsletter. But first, a story.

Hunters have always incorrectly referred to it as the "tag" draw. The MNRF has always referred to the Selective Harvest Program as a draw for a "Game Seal." Things have changed as of January 1, 2019.

I want to take a few minutes and share with you the experience of harvesting my first moose, which might have had a different outcome with the new regulations. Back in the days when the earth was young, pre-cell phone, if I recall correctly, the tag system for moose came into effect in the early 1980s. We hunt moose on the southern range of their habitat; originally in our area, moose season was every second year, and you needed two licenses to harvest a moose.

THAT DOG DON'T HUNT

Anyway, it was the first annual season, and the first draw for either an adult bull or cow. There was a lot of anxiety and no one was comfortable with the new system. Questions were asked amongst us. Could we still party hunt? Could anyone in the group fill the tags? What did we need to do with the tag? Where did it go? Would it stay attached if you were dragging the animal? Etc., etc…

The old adage rings true. "If you have two hunters arguing about the regulations you will end up with three different opinions."

I had a Cow tag, and one of the other hunters had a Bull tag. The tag/game seal was a self-adhesive semi-waterproof fold-over piece of paper. You applied for the tag through the mail, and if you were successful, your tag and a metal bracket arrived in the mail. You had to notch the tag with the time and date and immediately attach it at the kill site.

About an hour into the hunt on the Monday morning, I came across a moose about 100 feet away in a stand of mature hemlocks. Nice clear shot. I raised the gun looking through the scope. No horns! Relief! One less anxiety—I was going to fill my own cow tag.

When I approached the animal on the ground it was clear, all though it had no horns, it had an appendage—it was a bull.

I was unsure whether it should be tagged as a cow or bull. We cleaned it up and dragged to back to the camp and hung it on the game pole just in time for lunch. It was decided at lunch that I would drive into the closest MNRF office and get some clarification.

Everyone headed back out to hunt and I took my time getting cleaned up. When I headed out the door to my surprise, (now keep in mind that the camp was only accessible by a rough 4 X 4); there was a sea of green by the game pole… a green MNRF two-wheel drive half-ton truck, a green uniform worn by a green (rookie) CO.

After a two-hour inquisition and discussion, and my hand-written statement, the CO decided he would go back to the office and check with his superiors. He would be back on Wednesday.

The result of the Wednesday visit was a $275.00 fine for not applying the game seal at the kill sight and he confiscated the moose. Now it had rained for two days, the trail was a mess; I don't

103

know how he even made it into camp with the two-wheel drive. We dutifully helped him load the animal into the back of his truck, and he was on his way. He got about 200 feet from camp and got mired in the mud right up to the axles. We ended up towing him for the two miles out to the better road.

At that time any confiscated animals were donated to seniors' homes or to service clubs to utilize the meat. He indicated that my moose was going to the Shriner's wild game fund-raising dinner.

For years I was teased about how expensive my first moose was: to add insult to injury, not only did I have to pay the fine, and help tow it away, I had to pay $25.00 for a ticket to the Wild Game Dinner get a taste of my moose.

At least I got a picture of me with the moose.

From the MNRF newsletter:

New hunting regulations came into effect on January 1, 2019.

Here are two key changes:

Game seals are now called "tags."

Tags can be printed on regular white, letter-size (8.5"x 11") paper.

You are responsible for protecting your tag from weather and damage. It must be kept intact and readable at all times. We recommend using a plastic tag holder or a resealable plastic bag to keep tags clean and dry. This will keep the tag undamaged in case a Conservation Officer needs to inspect it.

You do not have to attach your tag and can instead keep the tag with you, *provided you are accompanying the animal or are immediately available to produce the tag for inspection.* You must securely attach the tag when you are no longer with the animal or immediately available to produce the tag for inspection.

By law, you must be in possession of the original tag that is provided at the time of purchase. It is illegal to copy, alter or modify your tag, except as required for notching.

Hunter reporting is now mandatory.

A simple and consistent mandatory reporting process for hunters is now in place.

Who has to report? All tag holders for moose, elk, deer, bear, wild turkey, and wolf/coyote have to report even if they didn't hunt or harvest an animal.

How do I report? You must submit your mandatory hunter report directly through the licensing service, either by automated telephone line (1-800-288-1155) or online, at https://www.ontario.ca/page/hunter-reporting.

When do I submit my report? You must submit your report at the end of your hunt or within 14 days of the close of the season.

What happens if I don't submit my report? Failure to report means you may be subject to penalties, including fines or restrictions on buying future licenses.

Will I still get a postcard? No. Voluntary postcards will no longer be mailed.

HAPPY HUNTING!

CHAPTER 28

Thunder the wonder dog

A while back, I shared the story of my first failed attempt to raise the best deer hounds in the district, the misadventures of Thunder 1, a female Beagle pound dog.

A few years had passed and I was still on a mission. I had kept the dog house and all the gear.

I was talking with a fellow hunter. He complained that during the past season he couldn't run his best hound because she was about to drop a litter of pups.

"Oh," I said, "what do you run—Black and Tan?" "No, beagles," he replied. Without checking with my wife, I blurted out "I'll take one of the pups."

"It's a deal! You can have the pick of the litter; they will be ready to go after Christmas," he replied.

I rushed home to share my excitement with my wife… she didn't share my enthusiasm.

When the time came to pick a dog, I was prepared. I had planned on taking home the biggest and most active of the females from the litter. Good breeding stock! There were six cute and cuddly pups curled up in the basket with the mother. Just as I was about to make my pick, the runt of the litter, a male, climbed out of the basket, stumbled over and lay on my foot. My heart melted. I named him Thunder.

THAT DOG DON'T HUNT

Thus began fourteen years of trials and tribulations. His exploits and attitude became local folklore.

I have to share a few stories from his first few months.

We had Thunder about three months and were in the throes of housetraining him. I built a barricade so he couldn't get out of the kitchen. We had just had expensive new plush slate grey carpet installed. My wife was in Toronto working the gift show and was to return the next evening; I slipped home for lunch to check on the dog. I was met by a bouncing puppy that was covered with and drooling what I thought was blood.

I continued into the house... it looked like an axe murderer had been at work, the barricade was down and there wasn't a square foot of the new carpet that wasn't smeared in various shades of red and there was little chewed up lipstick tubes littered everywhere. My wife had sold Avon at one time and had hundreds of small lipstick samples stored in the Vanity. Somehow, he had got to them. I don't think he missed one.

The dog would have to go and I would be in deep trouble when my wife came home to this mess.

I got on the phone and tried about four different carpet cleaning companies; everyone was too busy or didn't want to touch it... *"Lip stick? No, I don't think we can get it out,"* was the common theme. Finally, one individual consented; *"I can try and help you... I can come down from North Bay after supper. I'll have to charge you $50.00 for a service call and triple my regular rate."* I agreed without hesitation; I had to have it cleaned before my wife came home. I owe that gentleman a debt of gratitude. He worked through till the early hours of the morning cleaning the carpet, did a great job. The dog and I were saved. My wife would never know.

I next day I came home from work and greeted my wife. "How were things in the city?" "Great," she replied, "but the rug in the dining room is wet."

Another tale of his misadventures.

The phone rang on the Sunday morning after the deer hunt—it was the arena manager. *"Newman... you owe 50 cents for public skating... your dog is out on the ice."*

"Oh... thank god," I responded, "I'll be right down."

The back story...

Thunder's future as a hunting dog was in jeopardy; he had won over the hearts of the boys and wife and had settled in as a mischievous house pet. There were arguments about taking him hunting.

Fall arrived; he was still a pup... I wasn't hunting until the second week of the season, but I decided I would take him out at daylight on the first Monday; I could be back to the office for 9 am. We were about 200 ft off the south side of Hwy 124 when we came across a fresh set of deer tracks. Thunder had that natural skill or gift. He was pulling and tugging on the lead anxious to take off in pursuit. I was thrilled I had a hunting dog. I let him off the lead and he went off to the south baying away on the tracks. He went but a short distance and there was a yelp and the baying stopped. I whistled and waited for his return. Five minutes turned to ten and then twenty, all the while whistling and calling his name. I took off on his and the deer's tracks. I lost them both in a swale. I was concerned but... but not overly. He was a pup, but he seemed to be a natural; he would find his way back, I criss-crossed back and forth trying to cut his tracks—nothing.

I had a ten o'clock appointment at the office; I had to get back into town. My grandfather had told me, if you lose a dog, be patient, they will back track on their own. Leave your coat in a pile and they will likely stop at it. That's what I did. I really expected that when I got back in a couple of hours he would be curled up snoozing on the coat. NOT! I spent the next three days looking for him, put lost dog posters on every stop sign, checked at every house, and at night I called in on every hunt camp within a five-mile radius. I even let the kids miss a day of school and we scoured the bush where he had gone missing. Three days of lost income off work, searching. Nobody had seen him! I was devastated. I halted the search.

THAT DOG DON'T HUNT

On the Monday night I had to break the news to the wife and kids that Thunder had was gone. He had become a family pet. They were angry and heartbroken… no one talked to me for a few days.

Years later that I learned one of the hunt camps that I had stopped at, and who said they hadn't seen him, had actually picked him up on the highway about 10 o'clock on the Monday morning. They shot three deer in front of him; they said he was a great hunter.

They dropped him off at the arena on their way home on Sunday morning.

When I got to the arena, he was out on the ice enthusiastically chasing the skaters. He was doing a Bambi—his legs slipping out from under him. He was buff as could be, and in great shape.

It was a couple of years before I was allowed to take him hunting again.

Another time I will share more of his exploits.

CHAPTER 29

The Guy Who Almost Catches Fish

Let me preface my comments in this column: Hunters, as part of the culture, after returning to the cave from a successful hunt and at the resulting feast, were required, as entertainment and in celebration of the successful hunt, to tell of their bravery, skills, and expertise. In the telling of those stories, they were allowed, and expected, to embellish their exploits, and it was quite acceptable. From that time on, that tradition of storytelling has survived and flourished.

If I am wearing my hunter orange hat, then you know what I tell you is the gospel. The names, circumstances, location, and facts may be altered to protect the innocent. But it will be based on somebody's reality.

If a hunter tells you he got a ten pointer, you know he got a deer.

On the other hand, I have been told that fishermen cannot be believed, they are just plain outright liars. If a fisherman tells you he caught a ten pounder, you know he is lying, it was only two lbs.

If I have my khaki floppy fishing hat on, you should be a little skeptical of any fishing stories that I tell. Trying to change my fishing luck, I retired my floppy khaki and bought a new floppy camo hat, so you'll have to judge my stories for yourself.

THAT DOG DON'T HUNT

I have evolved as a fisherman. Back in the day I kept and ate what I caught... I evolved to catch and release, and this year, I have evolved to the point where I have skipped the catch phase.

My fishing fortunes set the pattern early in the year. Back in early January I headed out ice fishing on Lake Nipissing. I had just got to the hut, didn't even have my lines down yet, and I got a call about a family emergency, and had to head back to town. I didn't get back on the ice for a month. That time, I took two buddies with me; they caught a pile of perch and walleye... I got skunked! That was the first time in my life that I have been skunked on Nip.

With the floods this spring, I was late getting out on the water. My first trip out on the water set the pattern. I returned to the dock empty-handed. A couple of other fishermen arrived at the dock at the same time and were boasting and showing off their catch of great walleye.

I blurted out, "I almost caught a fish," and shared my story... I had hooked a huge Walleye, had to be 26 or 27 inches, six or seven pounds. No net! I got it up to the side of the boat and it got off.

Second venture out I hooked a trophy pike, fought it like a pro for about ten minutes, got it up to the side and it took a run under the boat, taking the line straight into the motor. You know what happened.

When I got back to the dock, I shared my story about another fish that got away.

It started as hushed whispers at the dock when I came in from fishing. *"That's Newman, the guy that almost caught a fish."* By mid-summer it was the everyday greeting at the camp. *"Hey Newman, how's the guy that almost catches fish?"*

I want to share with you a few of my experiences not catching a fish.

I went to Gull Island, the hot spot—no fish, but I got attacked by a flock of seagulls, and covered in white stuff.

I went to Pickerel Point, the go-to spot, five times. Nothing... not even a bite. In frustration, I scratched out the reference on the map, and scribbled, **NO FISH POINT!**

I got a call from a buddy. *"Newman, I hear you are not catching any fish, come up to Britt this weekend; I was slaying the bass last weekend."* He did again; on the four days we spent fishing together, he continued to pull in the fish on his side of the boat. Nothing on my side... We switched sides, but with the same results.

At one time, I enjoyed a cigar when I fished. Getting desperate to change my luck and catch a fish, I bought a $27.00 Cuban cigar. Just got my line out and settled into a troll. I lit the cigar; I was puffing away and relaxing... I snagged a huge fish. Fought it valiantly for what seemed like forever... finally my luck had changed; I was going to catch a fish, but no... Like any seasoned fisherman I was keeping the rod tip up, finally getting what had to be a ten lb pike to the side of the boat; I raised the rod up and toward me with both hands, the cigar still in my mouth. The line hit the ember of the cigar and away went the fish.

Mid-summer, the boys took pity on me. I got the call. *"Dad we have been limiting out all week; we will take you out tonight and you are sure to catch a fish."* We got to the hot spot and all three of us dropped our lines in. The jigs hadn't even reached the bottom—bang, bang, a double-header. One pulls up a whitefish and the other a lake trout. It was like that all night; they caught their limit, and I didn't catch a fish.

My grandson even recognized the gravity of the situation. A couple of weeks on my son asked him, "Can we take Grandpa out fishing again?" Reluctantly he replied, "Well okay, but if he is not catching any fish... you're taking him right back to the dock."

Late in the season, I took an elderly family friend out for a fish; he hadn't fished in 40 years. Sure, enough, he caught three really nice pickerel and a bass. I maintained my streak.

Another time out, I hooked a nice bass. It danced across the top of the water. It was exciting... got it to the boat and reached down to lip it. The rod bent with the tension, and just as I reached for the fish, the hook came out of its mouth and buried itself in the palm of my hand, right up to the shank. Again, no fish, but I did get a trip to Emergency.

THAT DOG DON'T HUNT

I could fill three columns with similar tales of woe. I tried every lure in the tackle box, every type of live bait, worms (even green worms), leeches and small, large, and extra-large minnows. I kept track, I used fourteen tanks of gas and countless hours on the water, but no fish.

That's the type of year it's been... *The year I almost caught a fish.*

CHAPTER 30

End of a chapter

I have a ring of keys—the camp keys… a key to the gravel pit gate, the main gate, the generator shed, the storage shed, the deadbolt, and the door knob. They have hung in a key box beside my front door in—let me count—seven, no eight, different houses for over forty years. I am not using them this year.

The "Howard Hunt Camp" gang is no longer. Age has taken its toll; I am the last surviving member of the original group. That chapter of my life has come to an end. However, life is like a good book that you can't put down. You want to quickly flip the page and keep reading to see what the next chapter brings.

I am on to the next chapter. I was invited to the "Gettin' Good Hunt Camp" back east in WMU 50 for the moose hunt. I was a little apprehensive. It was a chunk of bush I had never been in, and I didn't have a clue where I was going.

Just a heads up to the traditionalist. There wasn't a piece of wood to be found, everyone carried guns with synthetic stocks, either black or camo, myself included.

I was the new kid on the block, but the oldest. The rest of the gang are just one side or the other of forty, and have hunted together for a number of years; all but one of the others knew the bush like the back of their hands.

THAT DOG DON'T HUNT

As we stood outside in the predawn, getting ready to go, the hunt master began to give specific instructions to everyone. *"Marlie, you go by the big pine; Andrew, you go to "the" blue chair; Jay you go to the big hill, but don't go up it...* all meaningless to me, but everyone nodded in acceptance.

"Jimbo, follow the trail till it ends, go a little past that and you will come to two ribbon lines, take the left and go up to the blue chair." I'm confused! How far up is the end of the trail? How do you tell when you are at the end of the trail? None of these references made sense! They were all foreign to me. I was standing there looking at two different trails, and I was thinking… you just told Andrew to go to the blue chair. The confusion must have evident on my face. He went on to explain, "there are three chairs, 'the' blue chair, the 'second' blue chair, and the one on the ribbon line."

I started to chuckle to myself—I now had a little sympathy for the new hunters that over the years had joined us at the Howard camp. They must have been totally baffled.

Two sets of references had evolved over the years, one for the doggers and one for the guys on the stands. There were dozens of references. Most times, there were two different ones for the same location.

They all evolved from events or geography. I want to take a few moments and share some of them with you.

"When the run is over, leave your watches and we'll all meet up at the big old yellow birch." This seems simple enough! But the reality: back in the 70s, when we first started to hunt that particular chunk of bush, there was an old growth, hollow, yellow birch that towered over the rest of the trees, and was easily identified. Nature took its toll, and it blew down in the mid-90s. We cut it up for firewood, and there is no evidence of it ever being there, but we still met there and used it as reference up till the end.

"Line the guys up at calf landing." This was a common instruction. Over the years it was the most productive spot in the bush. We had harvested a number of moose, huge bulls and cows, but the first shot there was a calf and the name stuck. Now "calf landing" is not

115

a specific spot, but rather a half mile stretch along the road into the camp. But everyone seemed to know where to go.

"Follow the edge of the long beaver pond, hook right at the bear den, zigzag along the side hill, and you'll come out to the guys lined up on the flat rocks." Fairly easy instructions. However, in reality, it's almost a two-mile walk, the beaver pond has been dried up for twenty years, and no one has a clue where the bear den is. It now just refers to about a 10-acre patch of bush. Back in the 80s, on one of the coldest days of January, I was ribboning the property line and I came across an active bear den; I could see the hoarfrost rising from the den from a long way off. I actually took a look inside; it was only used once. The flat rocks stretch over a quarter mile.

Go to…

"the flat rock at the top of the hemlocks."

"the top of the hemlocks."

"the edge of the hemlocks."

Sounds confusing, and is if you're a newbie. They are three different locations, but all within about 300 feet of each other. There is a unique 75-acre thick mature stand of hemlock on top of a ridge. It's one of my favourite spots in the bush—it's as quiet as can be, the canopy is so thick the world seems to disappear, the ground is whaleback moss-covered rock, and the trees are so dense you can hardly walk through. But the moose and deer love it in there. When the animals bust out, depending on the wind direction, they seem to follow one of three routes. The flat rock on the east side, the top on the north and the edge on the west.

"Line up at the gravel pile" / "Line up at the gravel pit." Similar description, but 500 acres and three miles apart. To add to the confusion, *the gravel "pile"* does not exist. When we were improving the road into camp, we had a huge pile of gravel trucked in and stored along the edge of the road. It was there for about three years before we used it all.

I am looking forward to next year's moose hunt with the Gettin' Good Gang, and finding **the big pine, the blue chair, and the big hill**. I still don't know where they are.

CHAPTER 31

Stress and Anxiety!

I just finished filling in my mandatory online hunter's report on the Ministry of Natural Resources & Forestry website. My lack of computer savvy and computer crashes (three computers over two months) had created an elevated level of stress and anxiety with the whole new system. I was not looking forward to doing it. The hunters reading this will be aware, but for the rest of you, the MNRF instituted sweeping changes to the hunting licensing and tag process this year. According to the original press release, **"to modernize licensing products and approaches and improve client services."** If they were aiming for the bullseye, they were so far off target they didn't even hit the paper.

They introduced mandatory online or telephone license purchasing and game tag applications, along with mandatory hunter reporting—*failure to report on time carries a $300.00 fine for each species and effects your ability to get to get future licenses or tags.* The process has you purchase your online licenses and tags in the spring. Then after mid-August, you had to go back online and print your license summary and tags. You had one shot at printing your tags. Having heard horror stories of hunters having trouble with the printing process, I procrastinated as long as I could, fearing I would screw it up. The hunter is responsible for preserving the piece of paper from the weather. Printer ink and computer paper are not the most durable at the best of times. They suggested putting them in zip lock plastic bags. How environmentally friendly is that? I thought governments were advocating using less plastic. That's 300,000 plastic bags.

If you failed to print for whatever reason—a poor Internet connection, delay caused by lack of high-speed Internet service, issues with the MNRF website, or out of paper, you are forced to go to a regional Service Ontario office, go through a process, and have them print it. In my case, that would be an hour drive to North Bay.

My worry was about the impact it would have on my age group, but who knew; the younger generation whose smart phones and tablets seem to be an extra appendage, who do everything on their phones and can't function without them... Some don't have home computers or printers. If our camp was the norm, there was a mad scramble to find someone with a printer and then linking the cell phone up to that printer.

If you are sitting in a downtown Toronto office building and never been north of Hwy 7, these changes probably didn't seem too onerous. But it was devastating, decreasing the number of hunters of all ages. The last four gun shows I worked it was the main topic of discussion. *"I am not hunting this year because..."*

The MNRF estimates there are 100,000 moose hunters and 200,000 deer hunters in Ontario. It will be interesting to see how the new process affects those numbers.

For years, the MNRF has had a volunteer reporting process in place. They sent you the questionnaire and you returned it by mail. It was a little more comprehensive than the online version. Most years I filled it out. I always wondered if the MNRF even utilized the information, and now I question how they will use the mandatory info.

My grandfather used to say, "The only two things in life that are constant are death and change."

I am not opposed to change, but for what it is worth, I want to go on record: I am opposed to the new process, on number of levels:

Firstly, the social-economic impact: Hunting is one of the major drivers of northern Ontario's economy, and it is a social sport. In the past, you went into your local retailer to buy your license. (A side note, the MNRF never paid them enough to cover their costs.) While you were buying your licenses, you had an opportunity to talk to other hunters and the staff, you shared past hunting stories, and the forecast for the upcoming season. You also more than likely impulsively picked up shells, gloves, hunting accessories—anything in hunter orange or camo, etc.—even a new coat or a new gun. $$$$ into the local economy. That's gone!

Secondly: It penalizes those of us living in the north. Most rural areas don't have access to high speed Internet. Even telephone land lines are undependable, and cell coverage is limited.

Thirdly: With the new system and the mandatory reporting, the MNRF is victimizing, penalizing, and criminalizing hunters who fail to complete their paperwork (sorry, computer work).

On another level, filling out the hunter's report did allow me to realize how fortunate I am, and to recall the events of the hunt. I'll share those stories with you in the next column. I am dependent on my boys and the gang at the hunt camp to continue enjoying my hunting passion. To them a Thank You!

To those who know me, and have had to listen: at every opportunity, I am continually whining and complaining to anyone that will listen, *"I don't get to hunt and spend time in the bush as I use to."* Well… filling out the report, I realized that I didn't do too badly, three days of bow hunting, five days for moose, and nine days deer hunting. So, in the future, If you hear me whining, tell me to stop complaining.

I do recall in years past filling out the volunteer hunt report. Between the spring bear hunt, water fowl hunting, partridge hunting, fall bear, moose, and deer hunting, I logged nearly sixty days. At that time the info was sent and collated at the regional MNR office. I actually got a call from a friend at the office to verify the report.

My boys have inherited that passion for hunting. I take full responsibility. A shout out to my wife, daughters-in-law, and grandchildren for their continued patience, enduring our absences during hunting season.

Just as I was about to hit the Send button to submit my article, I received the MNRF quarterly online news letter. It contained the statement below.

"The ministry recognizes the significant changes to hunter reporting that came into effect in 2019. They understand that hunters need to adjust to the new reporting deadlines and overall process. The automatic license penalties will not be applied relative to the 2019 hunting season reporting requirements, as hunters familiarize themselves with these updates."

CHAPTER 32

Unintended Consequences

Last time we chatted, I complained about the MNRF Mandatory Hunter Reporting.

The principle of unintended consequences, often cited but rarely defined, is that actions of people—and especially of government—always have effects that are unanticipated or unintended.

The new regulations certainly proved that principle.

Anticipating the need to report my hunting activities, and not being able to rely on an aged memory, I decided I would keep an accurate log book of my hunting activities. In keeping with my nature, it ended up as post-it notes and scrap pieces of paper. I think I may have lied on my report... I found an extra post-it note that didn't get reported. Am I subject to a $300.00 fine?

As I sat down to write this article, I reviewed my daily hunting activities, the scribbled notes on the scrap pieces of paper that I had used to fill in the reporting form. It created the opportunity to clearly recall the events and happenings of the 2019 hunts.

I want to share a few of those stories, to tell you about a new subspecies of moose in WMU 50, a good judgement call (that may have created a new nickname), confirm it's true you can't teach an old dog new tricks, and about a chat with a bear.

As you may know, your moose license allows you to harvest a calf moose, and there is a draw for adult moose. We had a bull tag.

Let's start with the appearance of a new subspecies of elusive moose. They are the basis for most of the stories. The MNRF should do some genetic testing to confirm their existence and identify them. These new moose are either the smartest or luckiest in the bush. They proved that all week, time and time again.

Not an hour into the moose hunt, they appeared. For the readers who don't hunt, a 1200 lb. moose can tiptoe through the bush without making a noise, but when they are on a full run, the crashing and banging sounds like a train coming through the bush. My watch was in a patch of green bush with limited visibility… the freight train was heading straight for me. The adrenalin was pumping—I was excited! They must have got wind of me. They turned and angled away from me; all I could see was the black blurs behind the evergreens.

They did the same to the hunter on the next watch. Still on a full run, they headed on to the hunter at the next watch. As it turned out, there were four of the new subspecies of moose, single file, all nose to butt, with the calf leading the way, the cow next, and the two bulls pushing them. They were coming straight at him through the hardwoods. Literally straight at him. He had to jump out of the way to avoid getting run over. He elected not to shoot, concerned about accidently hitting the cow… good call. When they were a few feet away from him, I'm told he was waving his arms and yelling at them, "Stop… stop!" He was referred to over the next couple of days as "Stopper" or "Crossing Guard," but it didn't stick. This new breed of moose continued on to the last of our group, but he also wasn't able to get a shot at them. They continued over the ridge, passed two hunters from the abutting gang—they had a couple of shots at the calf but missed. These new breed of moose went by seven hunters, and continued unscathed on their way.

You can't teach an old dog new tricks. The next day I was in the same location… I was in a thick green bush on a little ridge with ravines on either side. On the south side, about thirty metres away, was a two-metre rock face that ran for about ten metres.

First, I have to explain I have always been a "wood stock and iron open sight" guy… switching to a red dot sight as my eyesight changed. For the first time, I was carrying a synthetic stocked gun with a reasonable quality scope. To focus through the scope, I couldn't wear my glasses.

I listened to the steady snaps and cracks in the bush as the moose headed toward me. I couldn't believe my luck... two days in a row. I couldn't see it, but it stopped on the top of the rock ridge. I was anticipating it coming down a gentle slope at the end of the ridge, and I turned my attention there. But no, it was one of the smarter new subspecies. I just caught the black blur in my peripheral vision—it jumped down off the two-metre rock face and there it stood. I could see the end of its snout and everything from the shoulders back, its head was obscured by maple saplings. The gun at ease, I inched toward it, weaving my head back and forth trying to see horns. It stood there for over a minute and I managed to get within fifteen metres and I still couldn't identify it. It slowly sauntered off... I was unable to get a shot. I shared the story at lunchtime, and my son piped up, *"Why didn't you look through the scope?"* **DUH!**

It repeated its trick, hiding its head from two hunters down the line.

Eight of those new smarter subspecies taunted us throughout the week, but finally on the last day, we were able to harvest a nice young bull of the old species.

For the first time in years, I didn't buy a bear license. A couple of days into the deer hunt, I had just got to my watch and off the ATV. I was in a beautiful stand of clear open mature hardwoods. I got a few metres from the bike and found a V-shaped black cherry to stand in front of to break my silhouette. Before I settled in, I made a 365 survey. Sure enough, off to my left and behind me I saw a huge black bear coming down a sidehill toward me. In no particular rush, it was just ambling along. It came up to the bike, just metres from me, and stopped. In a quiet voice I started to talk to it, and carried on a conversation. It hadn't winded (smelled) me and obviously couldn't see me, its attention focused on the noise. It raised it head, took a few steps toward me. I lost my nerve and yelled at it. It calmly turned and sauntered off the way it had come. That's the type of experience that keeps bringing me back to the bush.

CHAPTER 33

Skill or Luck?

I have a question.

I have been asking it of all the hunters I have encountered over the last couple of weeks. The answers have given me pause for thought. They were totally unexpected.

I asked. "If the success of a hunt was measured by harvesting an animal, would you rather hunt with a lucky hunter or a skilled hunter."

A recurring response that surprised me was that large number of the hunters asked immediately equated a lucky hunter with being an unsafe hunter. Not the case!

I am making a personal judgment call here in identifying the respondents: the average hunters replied *"the skilled hunter;"* the skilled hunters chose *"the lucky hunter."*

Hunters are under a lot of pressure; we are told over and over again that to be a successful hunter, we have to increase our skill level. Pick up any hunting magazine, and there is article after article telling us that, and offering tips on how to increase our skills. I have to admit I have bought into that concept and tried to increase my skills. But now I wonder.

Let's talk about a few cases of luck.

Every deer camp has that one individual, (you know who I mean)—there can be ten guys on watches and the deer comes out to him. Our camp refers to him as "the meat magnet." He makes no effort to be inconspicuous. He can be pacing back and forth to keep warm, answering natures call with his pants down, watching a couple of squirrels playing, sitting up against a tree having a snack. Whatever, but chances are the deer will come out to him. Is it luck?

It was not uncommon to have hunters stop in at the real estate office, and inquire about places to hunt. One of my salesmen and I had hunted 100 acres of crown land not far from town for the last couple of days with no success. In fact, we hadn't even seen fresh tracks. It was Saturday, and both of us had appointments at the office and had to work instead of hunt.

When I pulled into the office just before 8 am there was a truck sitting in the parking lot with a couple of obvious hunters decked out in hunter orange. They followed me into the office.

The driver asked, *"We left the south this morning at 4 am and have come up for a deer hunt. Neither one of us has deer hunted before and we have no idea where to go. Can you suggest some place to go where there are lots of deer?"* Disgruntled because I was working and not hunting, I was tempted to TELL THEM WHERE TO GO. Instead, I gave them a hand-drawn map and specific instructions.

They were back at the office before noon, all smiles and excited. *"We just wanted to stop in and thank you. We followed your instructions. We had just started walking up the hill, and were discussing which one of us would go up top and which one would go around. We didn't even have our guns loaded and this big buck was standing there. We fumbled getting our guns loaded, and deciding who would take the shot. It just stood there and watched us."*

They bought a hunt camp from me the next year, and turned into lifetime repeat clients and friends. So I guess both parties where lucky.

When I posed the question to a long-time friend and probably one of the most skilled woodsmen, fishermen, and hunters I know, his answer gave me pause. *"Animals sense and recognize a predator. They sense from the body language and movements of a skilled hunter... that they are a threat."*

THAT DOG DON'T HUNT

Why can't this happen in hunting season? It's a question I have asked myself over and over again. The occasions have been too numerous to count. Running a property line or doing a timber cruise, I have noisily walked up to an animal, and they just stand there unconcerned, watching me. I have even had them follow me as I continue along on my way. In hunting season, they would be gone in a flash.

Obviously, I didn't pose a threat.

The last few years my grandfather hunted—an extremely skilled hunter turned lucky—he was unable to do much walking, and had to give up the dogging, but wanted to enjoy a day in the bush. He would just take a watch. The first thing he would do was to find a comfortable stump to sit on, out in the wide open, no effort to conceal himself. He'd light a fire to keep warm and then stoke up his pipe. You could always tell where he was… you could smell his Old Sail pipe tobacco and see the smoke from his fire. Guess who the deer always came out to? He used to joke, *"If I knew deer hunting was this easy, I would have started doing this years ago instead of stalking them."*

When I look back, and I have told these stories before, luck played a major part in the harvesting of both my trophy animals. I was sitting on a fallen tree with an injured knee and eating a chocolate bar. The deer came up beside me from behind, on my tracks, and was intently watching the other hunters walk away. The moose appeared in very similar circumstances; the hunt was over, I had unloaded my gun, and was stretching my back when I heard the grunt behind me. I had to reload, turn around, and wait for him to raise his head. Strangely, although there were about twenty years between them, they were in the same spot, probably the last place a skilled hunter would want to be. Not much skill involved in either one.

One skilled hunter shared a story to confirm the luck theory. *"It was raining heavily, and I was dogging. I was soaking wet and decided to take a break. I sat under a hemlock tree out of the weather and lit up a smoke. I was sitting there just a few moments when a deer actually came up from behind, putting its head over my shoulder. It must have been following me."*

If I am relying on the meat, I'll take the lucky hunter any time!

CHAPTER 34

"Well let me tell ya now"

I want to try and paint you a picture!

It's a crystal-clear sub-zero winter night in the mid 1960s. The two brothers, Norman and Percy, have got together for their nightly visit, a session of reminiscing and storytelling. The sons of pioneers, they have been aged by a harsh life and environment. Years of hard physical labour, working, hunting, living in the bush, enduring the extreme seasons of northern Ontario, is evident in their leathered faces and in every body movement. Their thickset, solid stature verifies their Irish-Saxon heritage. They would be the first to tell you that even at their age, they could out-work any man half their age. They wouldn't be lying.

It's a squared log house built in the 1890s. The single pane windows are thick with frost. The kitchen wood stove is crackling as they sit on hard wooden chairs, one snuggled up to the fire box and the other beside the hot water reservoir on the other side of the kitchen stove. Their dress is the same, heavy wool mackinaw pants held up by wide suspenders, thick plaid flannel shirts with the sleeves rolled up, revealing the grey wool long underwear, and black rubber boots on their feet.

The ritual begins. They sit in silence. One starts to leisurely roll Daily Mail tobacco in a cigarette paper, and the other methodically stokes his pipe. Satisfied that they are encased in a haze of smoke, the hunting stories began. I would listen to the stories for hours. These two are responsible for my passion for hunting, and the development of what skills I may have had.

They usually started with "Do you mind the time," "It's as true as I'm sitting here," "Did I tell you the story," "Well, let me tell ya now," or "without a word of a lie."

Through necessity they had learned to be skilled hunters. They had learned from their Dad who, as a young child, emigrated from the slums of London with his parents to the wilderness of Muskoka district in the mid-1800s (at that time defined as the lands north of the Severn River and south of Lake Nipissing and the French River). They were lured by the appeal of free land grants and the glorified marketing. His Dad focused on carving a homestead out of the wilderness in the summer. In the winter, he was away at a logging camp. At a very young age, my great-grandfather was tasked with providing the family with game to eat. You either developed the skills or starved.

Percy started: *"Well let me tell ya now… Dad was one of the best trackers you ever did see… he used to tell us this story. He was just a youngster; it was late summer and they were out of meat. Gramma sent him out to get some venison. He came across a set of tracks from a huge buck. He was worried about that much meat spoiling before they could use it up. He decided to back track it. Yes siree, he back tracked it for two days and ended up shooting it when it was a fawn. Didn't have to worry about the meat spoiling."*

Hunting season was not defined by a date on a calendar, but by an empty cupboard and the ability to preserve what they harvested. They had a short window of opportunity, dictated by the weather. A venison carcass had to hang in the wood shed. No fridges or freezer. Nature was the freezer.

Deer hunting was wedged in between the first frosts of fall and before the deer disappeared to their winter yards. One unexpected heavy snow and you wouldn't have any winter meat.

Norman's turn: *"Percy, do you mind the time we got hell for taking two shots. Let me tell ya… you couldn't get to a store to buy bullets. Even if you could… you didn't have any money to buy them. Shells were expensive and precious. Dad used to load his own and was, stingy as all get out with the shells. He would only let you take a couple with you when you went hunting… you had to be darned sure you brought the used brass casin's home with you. It was goin' on late in the fall. Dad and Grandpa were getting ready to leave for the logging camp and sent us down to the lower pasture by the creek to see if we could find some venison. We were in our early teens; your grandpa carried that old single shot, breech-loading .577 Snider from the Nor-west rebellion that's hanging right there over the back door. I had Dad's old double barrel 12 ga with double-00 buck shot. We had split up and I came across a huge doe. It's as true as I'm sitting here… had to be 200 lb if it was an ounce… I took aim and fired. I know I hit it, but it still stood there. So, I up and fired again, and down it went. I had hit it both times. We dressed it out and set about dragging it home… it was so big the two of us could hardly drag it… we just got up by the barn and Dad come running, raisin' the dickens… mad as hatter he was. 'I heard two shots… how many times have I told you boys not to waste shells.' Yes sir, he was spittin' mad cause we had used two shots. Thought he would have been happy we got some meat."*

It must have been a lesson well-learned and remembered.

My Grampa saved up his pennies, and for his twentieth birthday in 1916, he bought himself a Winchester model 1894, 30WCF carbine with two boxes of shells, twenty to a box, from the Eaton's Catalogue. He used to boast that the gun was $19.99 and the shells were $2.00 a box. He passed the gun on to me in the late sixties, and there were still two shells in one box and three in the other. So, I am guessing… that would be 35 deer.

CHAPTER 35

Let's talk about nature

Not human nature, but Mother Nature, and how she provides.

Let me give you a few examples.

I have a **Sorbus americana** in my front yard. It is commonly known as the **American mountain-ash.** Hate is probably too strong a word, but that comes closest to describing my feelings for it. It's a love-hate relationship. I can never decide whether it is a tree, a shrub, or an out-of-control weed. It never gets any taller, just keeps spreading out. I read that in some places, it is favoured as an impenetrable hedgerow. It has serrated leaves, just like a knife; I curse it every time I mow the lawn. I end up scratched and bleeding. But I know it serves a purpose, even if it is just for one day, once a year, so it's safe from the chain saw.

The ash is half a season behind everything else in the yard. It's usually mid-July before the leaves are fully grown and it starts to flower. Clusters of small unremarkable white flowers produce clusters of small red berries that don't ripen till after all the birds have headed south in late October. They turn a dirty ugly brown, and they stay on the tree all winter—nothing touches them. There is a reason. The berries are not poisonous, but they are very bitter. I can remember trying them as a kid. Its now on my list of things not to do again. They are concentrated with malic acid, the same acid that causes apples to be tarty. But these berries are on steroids. There is only one bird that eats them, the early bird.

I look forward to the two symbols of the end of a long Canadian winter... maple syrup and sighting the first robin of the year. The syrup is in the freezer; now I await the Robin. Sure enough... on an early April morning as I stare out the window with my morning coffee in hand, watching the sunrise, there it is... its feathers all fluffed, shivering from the cold, sitting on the deck railing not ten feet from the ash tree, ignoring it—it's not time yet. But Mother nature's clock is ticking.

A couple of weeks on, I awake to six inches of fresh snow from a late spring storm. I am ecstatic... today is the day! By 10 o'clock a flock of robins have massed on the tree. I am thinking every robin in the district is here. COVID-induced boredom and idleness forces me to try to count them. I give up after reaching thirty. By dusk, there isn't a berry left on the tree. Today it has fulfilled Mother Nature's plan. I love that ash.

One of our homes was built on the site of an original homestead. It had a mature non-native plum tree in the front yard. It finally succumbed to old age and a mid-winter thaw and refreeze. It, too, fulfilled Mother Nature's plan. I had a healthier relationship with it. It was dazzling when it was in full bloom. Bright pink blossoms with an aroma you could appreciate a quarter mile away. The hummingbirds thought of it as their second home, and it always hosted a robin's nest. Year in and year out, it produced a bumper crop of inch-round bright red plums. As fall progressed, the fruit wilted and shriveled into... I guess, into small prunes. I have been told they even ferment a little. None of the summer birds would touch them. The fruit never fell off the tree and we purposely didn't pick them. We left them for a purpose. Just waiting for the day. Unlike with the ash tree, there was no specific event that triggered the birds. It could be anywhere from mid-December to mid-January, depending on having a long severe cold spell (now referred to as an extended Polar Vortex).

One morning, we would be awakened to a hellish racket, and they were there—the "Whisky Jacks." They hung around for a couple of days, drive us crazy with the chatter, strip the tree, and be gone… we wouldn't see them again for a year.

They are a hardy cold-weather bird. They don't migrate per se, but will congregate in the southern regions of their home range in mid-winter, looking for a snack.

The "Whisky Jack," or "Grey Jay," is now officially identified as the "Canada Jay." In 2016, it was named by Canadian Geographic as Canada's National Bird. I have been told the name "Whisky Jack" is an anglicized variation of the Cree or Algonquin name of "Wisakediak," referring to a trickster or camp robber.

My Grandfather used to tell stories of his time in the logging camps. *"Yes sir… I wouldn't of believed it if I hadn't seen it with my own eyes. Come late winter there was a couple of moose hanging around the camp to get away from the wolves. You would see them out in the swamp… Whiskey Jacks lined up in a row on their backs and others flying around them in a cloud…. never seem to bother the moose. Those birds would even land on the backs of horses we used for skidding. Made the teams really skittish and hard to handle."*

I have to admit I was always skeptical of the story. Thought it might have been induced by cabin fever after a long winter spent in the bush. I guess its too late to apologize.

A quick google search confirmed his story. The Whisky Jacks nest in late winter and there is documentation. They pick the blood engorged ticks off the moose and take them back to the fledglings in the nest, not for food but to act as miniature "hot water bottles" to warm the chicks.

Another example: Late in the fall when you are hunting, the leaves are all off the trees except for the oak and beech trees. The slightest breeze and the rustling of their leaves drives you to distraction. You are sure something is coming. I always have to keep reminding myself not to curse at them… they are part of Mother Nature's plan. They are there for a reason, they stay on the tree all winter. Come spring they act as the "big golden arches" in front of a

THAT DOG DON'T HUNT

fast-food restaurant. Those rustling leaves are a signal from Mother Nature to the bears coming out of hibernation, the deer retuning from their winter yards and all the other wildlife. She is whispering to them, my cupboard is bare, but I have left you some beech nuts and acorns—over here, come help yourself.

CHAPTER 36

Getting Ready

As you have heard me proclaim "ad-nauseam" in the past, my long-suffering wife maintains that at our house, there are only two seasons in the year, "hunting season" and "getting ready for hunting season."

Don't tell her, but she is probably right.

The provincial government, with the new procedures for purchasing hunting licenses online, has helped extend the getting-ready season. It usually takes me two stressful weeks of frantically searching to find the computer printouts for the licenses that I purchased on line back in the spring, and the game seals that I printed out in August. I know they are here some place. I put them away for safekeeping, but can't remember where I put them.

As I prepare for another season, I go through a mental checklist.

I mumble away to myself like some demented fool.

Found them! All my licenses, tags, and summaries are printed off the computer, and won't survive the outdoors. Have to find plastic Ziplock bags for each.

Small Game Licence for partridge? Check! Deer license? Check! Moose license? Check! Bear Licence? Wolf & Coyote license? Game seals? Six Licence Summaries? Firearms license? Check! Got them all. They are all safe and snug in their little plastic bags. You have to print off and carry a full-page license summary with each of the individual licenses. They are too bulky to carry in my wallet like I use to... where am I going to carry them in the bush so I don't lose them?

Let's see... got the trigger lock on my Savage Axis 308 calibre rifle that I use for moose, and the rifle is in a hard case. Case is locked. Got the trigger locks on my favourite deer gun, a Ruger 44 mag carbine, and a trigger lock on my 12-gauge shot gun. They are both in the two-gun hard case, and it's locked. Got the cable lock on the old 30-30 Winchester model 1894 my grandfather gave me. It's in a soft case, but you can't lock it.

I carry the old Winchester 94 that he bought back in 1916, just one day a year. At the camp on November 11, **Remembrance Day**, each year during deer season, we have what we affectionately refer to as a **"dirty thirty day."** I carry my grandfather's gun. My eldest son carries his maternal grandfather's gun. The other son carries gun given to by the family of his best friend who passed. Everyone at camp carries a 30-30 that was left to them. It's our way of remembering our heritage and honouring those before us.

Okay, I am just about ready to load the truck. Now where are the keys to each of these gun locks? Can't forget those! Oh yea! They are jingling in my pocket as I walk. I know it can't be coins... I never have any money left at hunting season.

Where is that new Hunter Orange vest that I had to buy? I was told last year that the blaze orange coveralls I had worn for years were not the right colour of orange, and I need 2,580 square centimetres (400 square inches) visible above the waist.

Man... I am worn out!

I stand back to rest for a moment and think back to simpler times, to a season over 55 years ago.

Now picture this!

I was a skinny 15-year-old kid! Yea, I know—no one believes I was skinny. On a Friday, I walked into the Canadian Tire store at Albion Road and Kipling Ave in Toronto. They had a sale on surplus World War 11 Mark 4, Lee Enfield 303 calibre rifles. They were in old battered wooden crates at the end of an aisle. In one crate, the untouched military rifles with full upper and lower wooden forestocks—some even had bayonets—on special at $10.00 each. The other crate was filled with sporter-ized, shortened forestocks at $15.00 each. No GST or PST.

I opted for a sporter-ized one because they were about four pounds lighter. The clerk helped me find one that was in excellent shape, and wasn't too scarred up. It had elevator sights on it for shooting out at distances, as opposed to the plain battle sights. It was the first gun that I had bought myself. I was set for the deer hunt on Monday.

No license was needed, no proof of age, no questions asked. I picked up two boxes of shells off the shelf, threw the gun over my shoulder, walked to the checkout, paid my money and walked home with it over my shoulder.

It gets even better!

The next day a (still skinny) kid, proud as can be, dressed in a red plaid jacket, and carrying a duffle bag and an un-cased 303 rifle, hopped on the TTC bus and rode across Wilson Ave from one side of the city to the other, over to Yonge Street at Hoggs Hollow, and waited around to catch the Grey Coach. The TTC driver had served in the second world war, and he reminisced about his days carrying an Enfield. He complained that they kicked like a mule...

I hopped on the Grey Coach bus and travelled four hours north, back home.

Not an eyebrow was raised, no SWAT team appeared, no fleeing masses, and no panic in the streets.

In fact, I had a conversation with an elderly lady that I sat next to, about how her late husband had liked to hunt.

The bus had a scheduled stop at Gravenhurst for a half-hour lunch break.

So! I can't leave my new prized possession on the bus? What do I do?

I carried it into the restaurant, leaned it up against the lunch counter beside me and quietly enjoyed my burger and fries.

Can you see this happening today?

Should it be able to happen again?

THAT DOG DON'T HUNT

I don't know.

Two things I do know!

First: the bus driver was right… the gun did kick like a mule.

Second: I should have bought three or four of the full-stocked surplus rifles. It would have been the best $10.00 investment I could have ever have made. They are collectors' items now, and sell for just under a $1,000.00 each.

CHAPTER 37

Foul Weather, Fowl Weather

Foul Weather…. Lousy, rotten, miserable, windy, cloudy, damp, rainy, sleety. **A good day to stay inside.**

Fowl Weather…. Lousy, rotten, miserable, windy, cloudy, damp, rainy, sleety. **A perfect day to go duck hunting.**

I am a duck hunter! I am a fanatic!

It's opening day. I am standing at the window watching the wind whip the driving sleet almost horizontally.

NO! NO!

What's the term used by Politicians these days when they tell an untruth? "I misspoke."

Let me restate that… I used to be a duck hunter. As I started to punch the keyboard, I just realized that it's been years since I hunted ducks. Age has convinced me to go with the "Foul Weather" definition.

You can't just go out to the closest marsh and hunt ducks… You need a federal firearms license, (PAL), a Provincial hunting license, a small game license, and you must have a valid federal Migratory Game Bird Hunting Permit with an affixed Canadian Wildlife Habitat Conservation stamp. Duck hunters have to use non-toxic or steel shot shells. The costs keep climbing.

THAT DOG DON'T HUNT

Duck hunters are special! They are a breed unto themselves. I have been asking just about everyone I met over the last week. *"How would you describe a duck hunter?"* Some of the responses: Fanatical, Passionate, Obsessive, Committed, Crazy (should be committed).

How do you describe someone that gets up in the middle of the night in the worst weather, spends hours setting up their decoys in the dark, sits shivering in their blind, cold and damp, waiting till sunrise for ducks that may or may not appear? Regardless of the outcome, with great enthusiasm, on the way home says, *"I enjoyed that… it was fun."*

How do you describe someone that spends the off season driving their spouse to distraction practicing their duck call skills? Someone who obsesses over whether to use a one or two-reed call. Has a garage full of decoys, camo netting, an unlimited rack of camo clothing, two or three portable duck blinds, a camo'd boat and motor, but no room for the wife's car.

According to Wikipedia:

Waterfowl hunting is the hunting of ducks, geese, and other waterfowl for food and sport. Many types of ducks and geese share the same habitat, have overlapping or identical hunting seasons, and are hunted using the same methods. Thus, it is possible to take different species of waterfowl in the same outing. Waterfowl can be hunted in crop fields where they feed, or more frequently, on or near bodies of water such as rivers, lakes, ponds, swamps, sloughs, or oceanic coastlines. (I have duck hunted all these locations)

Hunters position themselves in camouflaged blinds, either on land or water, to conceal themselves from waterfowl, and use decoys to entice the birds near rivers, lakes, ponds or in fields planted with crops, as waterfowl have sharp eyes and can see colors. Waterfowl hunters also often use retriever dogs to retrieve dead or injured birds in the water. Hunters also may use a boat to get downed birds.

The ducks have keen eyesight, but the hunters have even better—they have to identify the species as it flies overhead at 80 kph. They have to make a judgment—is it a black, mallard, canvasback or teal duck?

Ducks have a lot of political clout. Back in 1917, one of the first bilateral agreements with the United States was the **Migratory Birds Convention Act (MBCA)**. It was significantly updated in 1994, and contains regulations to protect migratory birds and their habitat from destruction by wood harvesting, hunting, trafficking, and commercialization.

Ducks have lots of friends—if they call people who shoot at them "friends." The largest waterfowl conservation and habitat protectors are hunter-lead groups like DUCKS UNLIMITED and DELTA WATERFOWL. Their efforts with habitat restoration and protection not only benefits the ducks and wildlife in general, but us humans as well. Marshlands are nature's filters, and their protection creates cleaner air and water for all. The magnitude of the efforts of these organizations is astounding. Their annual budgets are north of $100 million dollars, and over the years, they have helped with the rehabilitation of almost 200 million acres of land. That is more than six times the total area of the combined provinces of Nova Scotia, New Brunswick, and Prince Edward Island.

Duck hunters have their own language.

A decoy is known as a *block* (a carry-over from the days when decoys were made of blocks of wood), *spread, rig, or set*. *Fully flocked decoys* have nothing to do with a flock. Its a method of, now, using mechanically moving decoys, or the old-fashioned method of adding cloth to the decoys to make them appear alive.

When a duck is gliding into the decoys to land it is **locked up**, **cupped up**, or **feet down**. When it is hit it **folds up**, an active day of birds is a **flight day**.

A bright warm sunny day with no ducks is a **Bluebird Day**.

The bird dog has a **soft mouth** (can carry the prey back without damaging it), and is **"biddable"** (willing to learn).

Speaking of dogs… every duck hunter I have met will argue they have best trained, most intelligent, faithful, obedient, loving retriever in the area, if not the country.

There are six recognized breeds of retrievers. They all share the same characteristics: intelligence, solid build, versatility, a gentle and pleasant nature, willingness to learn, and a desire to please, and they are great companions. In Duck language, **biddable**.

When I was facilitating Media Awareness seminars for Gun Clubs, I used to tell this story to demonstrate the bias of the media against hunting and guns.

Mac had purchased a new Retriever pup, and had spent a year training it. Opening day was at hand, and he wanted to show off and share the expertise of his dog.

He calls his buddy. *"Charly, opening day is Saturday, come duck hunting with me and see how well I have trained this pup. You are not going to believe it."*

The two are sitting in the duck blind, the pup sitting obediently and attentively at its master's side. Two ducks fly over, and both Mac and Charly knock one out of the air. The pup just sits there. Mac said *"Now watch this."*

He gives a hand signal and the pup leaps out of the blind, gets to the water's edge and just skips across the top of the water, picks up the one duck, makes a sharp turn, skips over and picks up the other duck, and then skips over the water back to the blind.

Charly is dumbfounded. "That dog is incredible, not only did it bring both ducks back, but it walks on water. You have to share this with the world. My nephew just started writing in the sports section for a big city newspaper; let's bring him out and he can write the story and let everyone know this dog walks on water.

The reporter comes out mid-week and he is awestruck. He can't believe what he is seeing. He takes picture after picture. With excitement he says, *"This is going to make my career! The whole world has to know about this dog; he walks on water! I have enough material for a full-page article. I'll get it in to my editor tomorrow—he has the last say on what is printed. It should be on the front page of the sports section this weekend!"*

Anticipation is building all week for the article. The hunter has called all his friends and relatives, making sure they are going to pick up a paper. Saturday arrives, and he stays home from duck hunting; he rushes down to his local convenience store to pick up the paper.

He discards everything but the sports section… disappointment! Nothing on the front page! Frantically he searches through the rest of the section looking for the article. There it is! Quarter page, second last page, down in the left corner (least desirable location). Big Bold headline…

DUCK HUNTER'S DOG CAN'T SWIM!

CHAPTER 38

Who Knew?

"If we are going to effectively represent hunters and gun owners, the first thing we should do is find out who they are, how involved they are, and what their concerns are," I suggested in a development session for the Canadian Firearms Institute.

The group cobbled the money together, out of our own pockets, to have a professional market survey completed.

The answers astonished me. They will astonish you.

The survey said:

Less than three-quarters of 1% of them belonged to any organization to protect their interests. Those that did, belonged to three or more organizations. Based on those figures, if someone tells you that Canada has a strong gun or hunting lobby, you can call them a "fisherman," as defined in the Hunt Camp Porch Dictionary.

Hunters represented the largest number of volunteers and the most generous financial supporters in any and all conservation groups. We realize that, to ensure that we and our future generations are able to continue the sport and the tradition, and enjoy the fruits of the hunt at the table, it's in our best interest to protect wildlife.

The demographics revealed that respondents were predominately male, over 40 years of age, weighted heavily in the 55-plus age group (that would be me). They had above the national average level in education, above average annual income, and they tended to be professional or self-employed. I might add, there were a disproportional number of accountants.

Later studies indicated a dramatic change, with a large increase in the 20 to 30 age group, and a noteworthy increase in the number of women hunting.

Politically, they are not of like minds. Their voting patterns echoed those of the general population, and they seldom voted for issues that affected their sport.

A research paper prepared in 2018 by The Conference Board of Canada, "The economic footprint of Angling, Hunting, Trapping, and Sports Shooting in Canada," presented to the Ontario Federation of Anglers and Hunters (OFHA) and the Canadian Sporting Arms and Ammunition Association (CSAAA), revealed the importance and economic impact of hunting.

Respondents to the study were asked, *"What is your primary motivations for hunting?"* The top three answers, in order, were: 1) recreation and enjoying the outdoors, 2) enjoying family/friends/tradition, and 3) food and sustenance. Of the respondents to the study, three quarters hunted for food and sustenance.

The study indicated that there were over 1.3 million hunters in Canada; that's more than the 1.2 million adults that play hockey.

The research paper included questions about the amount of spending on gas, travel, accommodations, clothing and gear, and firearms and ammunition, as well as major purchases like ATVs and boats, etc.

Hunters spent over $5.9 billion on hunting, with a resulting total impact on GDP of $4.1 billion. Hunting supported 33,000 jobs, which represents just under $2 billion in labour income.

Boring stats... but significant. I am going to repeat that. Hunters yearly pump **over $5.9 BILLION** into the Canadian economy. In rural Canada, hunters are a driving force of the local economies.

With the uncertainty and frailty of our food supply chain, and the quality of that food emphasized by the COVID-19 pandemic, I am sure hunting will become more prevalent and more necessary.

If you are a hunter, or you want to learn more about hunting, I have listed the Provincial organizations. Their mission statements have a common thread.

They are non-profit organizations dedicated to fostering awareness and enjoyment of our natural resources. They promote the sustainable use of those natural resources through education and proper wildlife management.

Join, make a donation, and help ensure the survival of our heritage. Their contact info is listed at the end of the book.

PROVINCIAL WILDLIFE, HUNTING AND FISHING ORGANIZATIONS

Newfoundland and Labrador Wildlife Federation (NLWF)

St. John's, Newfoundland and Labrador
http://www.nlwf.ca/

The Nova Scotia Federation of Anglers and Hunters

P.O. Box 654,
Halifax, NS
B3J 2T3
Phone: (902) 477-8898
https://www.nsfah.ca

New Brunswick Wildlife Federation

P.O. Box 549
Moncton, NB
E1C 8L9
nbwildlifefederation.org

Prince Edward Island Wildlife Federation

PO BOX 692
SOURIS, PE, C0A 2B0
420 University Ave.
Charlottetown, Prince Edward Island
(902) 892-3332

Fédération québécoise des chasseurs et pêcheurs

F 162, rue du Brome
Saint-Augustin-de-Desmaures (Québec)
G3A 2P5
(418) 878-8901
info@fedecp.com

Ontario Federation of Anglers and Hunters

4601 Guthrie Drive, PO Box 2800
Peterborough, ON
K9J 8L5

Phone: 705-748-OFAH (6324)
F: 705-748-9577
https://www.ofah.org/

Manitoba Wildlife Federation
Email: info@mwf.mb.ca
Phone: (204) 633-5967 / Toll-free (877) 633-4868
Address: 4-999 King Edward Street, Winnipeg, Manitoba
R3H 0R1

Saskatchewan Wildlife Federation Central Office
9 Lancaster Road
Moose Jaw
SK S6J 1M8

(306) 692-8812
https://swf.sk.ca/

The Alberta Fish and Game Association
13045 – 156 St NW,
Edmonton, Alberta, Canada
T5V 0A2

780-437-2342
office@afga.org

BC Wildlife Federation
TOLL-FREE: 1-888-881-2293
PHONE: 604-882-9988
FAX: 604-882-9933

101 - 9706 188 Street
Surrey, BC V4N 3M2
https://bcwf.bc.ca/

Yukon Conservation Society
302 Hawkins Street,
Whitehorse, Yukon, Y1A 1X6

Tel: 867-668-5678
Email: info@yukonconservation.org

Canadian Wildlife Federation
Canadian Wildlife Federation (Ottawa - Head Office)
c/o Customer Service
350 Michael Cowpland Drive
Kanata, Ontario K2M 2W1
mailto:info@cwf-fcf.org

1.800.563.9453
http://canadianwildlifefoundation.org/

Ducks Unlimited Canada

PO Box 1160
Stonewall, Manitoba, Canada
R0C 2Z0

1 800 665-DUCK (3825
https://www.ducks.ca

Delta Waterfowl Canada

Unit 200-1765 Sargent Avenue
Winnipeg, MB
R3H 0C6

1-877-667-5656
Email: canada@deltawaterfowl.org

CPSIA information can be obtained
at www.ICGtesting.com
Printed in the USA
BVHW030239090122
625753BV00004B/258/J

9 781525 597282